GREEN IS THE NEW BLACK

GREEN IS THE NEW BLACK

INSIDE AUSTRALIA'S HARDEST WOMEN'S JAILS

JAMES PHELPS

EBURY
PRESS

An Ebury Press book
Published by Penguin Random House Australia Pty Ltd
Level 3, 100 Pacific Highway, North Sydney NSW 2060
www.penguin.com.au

Penguin
Random House
Australia

First published by Ebury Press in 2017

Addresses for the Penguin Random House group of companies can be found at
global.penguinrandomhouse.com/offices.

National Library of Australia
Cataloguing-in-Publication entry

Phelps, James, author
Green is the new black: inside Australia's hardest women's jails/James Phelps

ISBN 978 0 14378 281 0 (paperback)

Women prisoners – Australia
Female offenders – Australia
Reformatories for women – Australia
Prisons – Australia
Prison violence – Australia
Prison psychology – Australia

Cover design: Luke Causby/Blue Cork
Cover image: AdobeStock
Internal design and typesetting by Midland Typesetters, Australia
Printed in Australia by Griffin Press, an accredited ISO AS/NZS 14001:2004
Environmental Management System printer

Penguin Random House Australia uses papers that are natural, renewable
and recyclable products and made from wood grown in sustainable forests.
The logging and manufacturing processes are expected to conform to the
environmental regulations of the country of origin.

Contents

1

WELCOMING A WOMAN

Scream, Bitch

The teenager scratched, slapped and screamed.

'Get the fuck off me,' she shouted. 'Guard. *Guard!* Help. Someone. *Please!*'

The man she was hitting tightened his grip, the tips of his fingers turning white as they pressed into her delicate throat.

And then he laughed.

'Scream, bitch,' he said, the smell of his breath as foul as his face. 'Scream as much as you like. They can hear you – everyone can. But guess what? They don't care. They brought you to me, didn't they?'

His tongue slid from his mouth, the pink flesh curling before slithering across his lips. 'In fact,' he continued, a fresh slick of saliva cooling his cracked grin, 'they are going to have a turn too.'

He sucked on his tongue, returning it to the dark hole from which it came. He stood and stared. All still.

And then he struck.

His heavily tattooed hand gripped the back of her head, his fingers, etched with jailhouse ink, taking a fistful of blonde. Then he swung, sending her head smashing into the cement wall.

The young woman fell to the floor, slumping and sobering up instantly on the cold, hard tiles.

She was down – certainly dazed and dented – but not out.

Oh, how she wished the blow had knocked her out cold.

She looked up and there he was. The well-known Sydney criminal smiled as he pulled down his pants . . .

Earlier . . .

Still in a drug haze, the dishevelled girl smiled as the magistrate sentenced her to jail. Departing, she flicked her sun-bleached hair from her face. Young, pretty and unmarked, she looked like a schoolgirl. Everything was normal, except for her eyes. They were vacant. A lake of placid blue, oblivious to fear or consequence.

Oh . . . if only she knew what was to come.

'I had no idea what I was in for,' the girl, now a grand-mother who has spent more than 20 years of her life in New South Wales jails, recalled. 'I don't think I even cared that I'd been sent to jail. It didn't mean a thing. I wasn't scared. Nothing like that.'

But soon she was . . .

'I thought I was on my way to a farm,' she said. 'Or to something like a very strict school. A home for bad girls.'

Only she wasn't.

'Out,' said the prison escort, his baton poking her ribs. 'This is us. We're here – Grafton Jail.'

Grafton? What the fuck? GRAFTON?

She looked up, the methamphetamine that put her in this mess still swimming in her veins.

'Nah, not me,' she said, rubbing her eyes. 'This is Grafton. This is a men's jail.' She pointed down at her ample breasts. 'Tits. See? I am not a man. I think we should be heading down the freeway to Sydney now.'

The prison escort deadpanned. 'No, love. This is you. Off you get.'

The woman's voice strained as she remembered, now 30 years on, the horror of arriving at the notorious jail. She still has nightmares about the towering sandstone walls of Grafton Correctional Centre that welcomed her to one of Australia's most notorious prisons.

'I thought I was on my way to a women's jail in Sydney,' she said. 'But I came from up on the North Coast of New South Wales, and there were no women's jails up that way. They would take women like me to Grafton on remand while they worked out where to send us.'

Grafton? Of all the jails in Australia. It had to be Grafton.

'I knew about the place,' she said. 'Everyone did. That's where they sent the "tracs". The worst of the worst.'

Yep. The most troublesome prisoners in New South Wales were sent to Grafton Jail. Men they called the 'intractables'.

Some of the most violent men in Australian history had called this house of horrors home – killers like Neddy Smith, John Stuart and Archie McCafferty, to name but a few.

Justice John Nagle exposed Grafton's long history of abuse in the Nagle Royal Commission, held from 1976 to 1978, stating:

'It is the view of the Commission that every prison officer who served at Grafton during the time the jail was used for intractables must have known of its brutal regime. The majority of them, if not all, would have taken part in the illegal assaults on prisoners.'

Grafton was the home of the 'reception biff' – a vicious beating given to new inmates as a painful prison welcoming.

'In some instances the beatings even began before the security belt and handcuffs were removed,' continued Nagle. 'The beatings were usually administered by three or four officers wielding rubber batons. The prisoner was taken into a yard, ordered to strip, searched and then the "biff" would begin.'

But surely this girl – all skin and bone, just a sun-tanned teenager from the Surf Coast – had nothing to fear?

'I wasn't so sure,' she said. 'But yeah. I wasn't expecting to cop a beating. Nothing like that.'

And she wasn't belted. There was no reception biff. What happened to her was far worse . . .

The girl was processed. She was stripped and searched.

'It was terrifying,' she said, 'but all pretty standard practice, now that I can look back with way too much experience.'

She was taken to her cell, all intimidating stone blocks with a heavy steel door. She slumped down on her new bed – a rock-hard piece of foam with an equally uncomfortable pillow that felt like it had been filled with sand instead of feathers.

The drugs were fading fast, the lingering high becoming a creeping sick. The comedown. She began to shake as she attempted to find sleep.

'*Coming* in!' announced a guard after banging on the door.

He waited, giving the girl time to dress if she happened to be naked, before swinging the steel door open.

She rubbed her eyes, the blue now swallowed by a sea of rising red.

'What?' she said. 'What do you want?'

The officer stood by the door. 'Off to see the nurse. Time to get you checked out.'

She shuffled from her bed and joined the guard in the hall.

'The nurse was there waiting,' she recalled. 'He was a male nurse, and I thought I could trust him. I'd just been sentenced and had gone through reception. I thought it all must have been part of the program.'

It wasn't.

The trio travelled to the clinic, everything silent except for the sound of their feet as they shuffled across the ancient Grafton sandstone.

They stopped in front of a double door; steel but for a perspex viewing window. The guard pulled his keys from his belt and snapped the lock.

'In here,' he said, pointing towards a bed.

She walked through the open door and into the room.

Crack!

The door slammed shut. Neither the guard nor the nurse had followed her inside.

Ting! Ting!

Keys rattled on the other side of the reinforced steel door.

Click!

The lock sprung back into place.

'I looked through the window and asked what was going on,' she said. 'The nurse was walking away.'

The guard shrugged before turning and leaning back against the perspex and steel door.

'Howdy.' The silence in the room was broken by a voice beyond the bed. 'Why don't you come and have a little lie-down over here.'

The woman turned away from the door, from the indifferent officer standing guard on the other side.

She looked towards the beckoning man. He was no nurse. No guard, either. No, this man was an inmate – in fact, he was an intractable. A violent, hardened criminal with a reputation as long as his rap sheet.

'He was the nurse's sweeper [an influential inmate who has special privileges],' she recalled, referring to the inmate and his job of assisting the male nurse. 'I knew who he was. Everyone knew who this guy was.'

But what did he want?

'It was obvious,' she said. 'He wanted to rape me.'

The inmate, who will remain unnamed given he is deceased and unable to respond to the accusations, walked slowly towards the girl.

'How about you come over here and give me a bit of a kiss,' he said. 'Come on. Let's have a bit of fun.'

The withdrawal shakes from the meth were now tremors of terror.

'No, thanks,' she said. 'I'm just here to see the nurse.'

The short, stocky man, all prison-yard muscle, walked towards the woman, quickly closing the gap.

Bang! Bang! Bang!

She bashed against the door, slamming the underside of her tightly clenched fist into the steel three times.

'Let me out,' she yelled. 'HELP!'

The officer on the other side remained still. Silent.

'He ain't going to help you,' said the inmate. And then he grabbed her by the hair and smashed her head into the wall, the blow sending her crashing to the floor. Stunned and terrified, she looked up at her attacker. He was now holding his penis, which was angry and erect.

A rush of adrenaline broke her from her momentary paralysis and she lashed out. She kicked with both legs, hitting him in his knees. His pants, slumped around his ankles, turned trip-wire and he crashed to the floor, cock in hand.

'And I got up and I ran,' she remembered. 'And I screamed. Screamed as loud as I could. I ran to the other side of the room and I could see a big window. I went over and it looked out into the visiting area. I could see a couple of guards there, and I screamed and banged. As loud and as hard as I could.'

The would-be rapist rushed across the room. She screamed louder, banged even harder.

'He was just about on me when one of the guards in the other section looked towards me,' she said. 'I managed to catch his attention.'

The officer hit the alarm and the attacker stopped in his tracks.

'Oh well,' he said as he put his penis back in his pants. 'We'll have to finish this later.'

He receded back into the shadows.

'The guards rushed in,' she said. 'The guard and the nurse who had locked me in were there too. The only way I got out of it was by screaming.'

She dared not make a complaint; the co-conspirators stared daggers at her as the guard who raised the alarm asked her to explain.

'I knew better than that,' she said. 'I didn't know how long I would be locked up in this hell hole before I was moved. I didn't want the guard going after me later.'

Former prison officer (PO) Roy Foxwell was in charge of Grafton Jail shortly before the alleged attack, and for a period after.

'I don't think I was there that particular year,' Foxwell said. 'I was moved down to Sydney for a while. But, yes, we did have a small number of women in the jail at most times. I don't know this particular woman, but I know the inmate she was referring to. It certainly wasn't beyond him, and he had form with sexually assaulting women on the outside. He was certainly a predator.'

Foxwell doubts any of the officers he worked alongside with would have been complicit in an attempted rape.

'I would be surprised if the guards had been involved,' Foxwell said. 'Especially in a small place like Grafton was back then. We didn't have the outside jail built yet, and it was a very confined place she is talking about. It was just a room called "the clinic", even though it wasn't much, where the male nurse operated from. He would have had a sweeper, so that could be correct.'

Foxwell described the women as being worse than most of the intractables – the hardened scum sent to Grafton because they couldn't be dealt with anywhere else.

'[The women] weren't there for a long time,' Foxwell continued. 'As soon as they were sentenced we would sling them down to Sydney. Most of them were pretty rugged women, very ordinary types. Now and again you would get one that was reasonable, not a real hard crim, but that was rare because most of them had form.

'They were all North Coast girls, and they were in and out for most of their lives. To be honest, they were a pain in the arse more so than any of the other prisoners in the jail. They caused a lot of trouble even though there would only be a few of them. They were kept in a separate area that was more like rooms than cells. But despite how difficult they were I never saw an officer lay a hand on them.'

This girl survived an eight-week stint in Grafton before she was handcuffed and thrown into the back of an old diesel truck. She vomited during the nine-hour trip from Grafton to Sydney, the noxious fumes sending sick slapping to the floor. She also pissed her pants, the driver never stopping to let her use the toilet. Finally, the door swung open and she faced her new hell – a place called Mulawa, the meanest female lock-up in the land. Grafton would soon look tame, those tattooed male inmates nothing compared to Australia's worst women – who bashed, raped and killed.

In the following pages you will find the uncensored accounts of those who have served time, either as inmates or officers, in Australia's hardest women's jails. And forget everything you know. This is not the popular Australian TV series *Wentworth*. Nor is it the global hit *Orange is the New Black*. No, this is worse; at times, incomprehensively so. You will meet the women of your darkest nightmares, and for just a while, if I have done my job properly, you will be locked up with them.

We will start with the no-holds-barred, on-the-record account from a first-time offender who would find herself locked up with three of Australia's most infamous female killers.

Welcome to Hell – a place where Green is the New Black.

The Model Inmate

The woman walked over to the only toilet in the jam-packed Surry Hills police station holding cell. There were now 17 women locked away in this tight concrete space, standing room only. Without a barrier to screen the toilet from view, not so much as a curtain, the other 16 women could only look away to avoid watching the newest inmate as she pulled a tampon out of her vagina. She bled into the toilet, urinated and, when finished, stood up, unwrapped a fresh tampon and inserted it.

But she wasn't done.

No, she started pushing. She strained and clenched her arse cheeks. The rest of the cell couldn't help but turn for a look as she moaned in pain. And then she stood up, a full-frontal view for all, before reaching around to stick her hand up her bottom. The late-night addition to the inner-city watch house pulled something out. But nobody could quite make out what yet. *Or maybe they just weren't looking too hard?*

'Anyone want an eccy?' she shouted while removing a bulging wad of cling wrap from the plastic M&M's container she had been hiding up her arse.

A former *Penthouse* pet stood in the far corner, watching on in horror as each and every girl in the cell went up and collected an ecstasy tablet from the now very popular menstrual smuggler.

In jail for the very first time in her life, the model, movie extra and sometime stripper and men's magazine star was scared stiff. She sat on the floor, grabbed her knees and started to shake.

Get me the fuck out of here.

Victoria Schembri was 32 in 2009 when she was sentenced to serve a maximum of seven years in jail for claiming more than $500,000 worth of bogus GST refunds. The mother of three was convicted of 17 criminal counts, including dishonestly obtaining a financial benefit by deception, attempting to obtain a financial benefit by deception, and dealing with the proceeds of crime, after her signature was found on fraudulent business activity statements (BAS).

A complete 'clean-skin' until she and her co-conspirator bikie ex-husband were busted for fraud – she had never been in a police station, let alone a cell.

But now here she was, her designer clothes removed, her expensive jewellery confiscated, dressed in prison green and shaking uncontrollably on the cold concrete floor of the police cell.

'My first experience in a jail cell was just horrific,' Schembri said. 'I was thrown into a place they called the "dog box", a lock-up at Surry Hills [Police HQ].'

Schembri was escorted to the cell in the late afternoon. She had just been sentenced for the role in the crime she claims to have had nothing to do with.

'There were only two women in that cell at first,' Schembri said. 'They were off their faces on drugs and just fucked up.'

But soon other women arrived, one at first, then two – eventually the cell was chock-full of dishevelled drug addicts, and one dealer who had an M&M's container hidden in her arse.

'Before I knew it there were 17 women in the cell,' Schembri recalled. 'There was absolutely no space at all. I gave up my seat at some point because I was terrified. I stood because I didn't want to get bashed for a chair.'

Schembri was nothing like the other women in the cell – the tattooed, bruised and even bloodied criminals who were telling her she was 'real pretty' and touching her hair.

'I just kept my mouth shut,' Schembri said. 'I'd never been around people like this, and I didn't know what their intentions were. I didn't want to have a thing to do with them, and I worked my way into the corner and stood by myself.'

Suddenly the cell erupted.

'Fuck yeah,' yelled a woman with arms covered in sores. 'I'll have a *biccy*.'

They were all soon pushing towards the woman with the drugs, shouting and clapping as they kickstarted an impromptu prison cell party.

'It was disgusting what had happened,' Schembri said, 'watching her as she got them out. She obviously had her period because she pushed a tampon up in front of us. But then she suddenly started to push something out. It wasn't coming out of the front door, obviously, because she was all plugged up.

'She spat out this mini M&M's container full of ecstasy. She asked anyone if they wanted one before handing them all out.'

Why would anyone give away about $1000 worth of drugs? Why would they risk smuggling in contraband just to give it away?

'Good question,' said Schembri. 'I guess she just wanted to make some friends. Maybe she had some enemies inside and wanted back-up.'

Schembri sat in the corner and shook.

Maybe I need to make some friends. Do I have any enemies?

Schembri spent four days in the horror house at Surry Hills. New women came, and other women went. To her they all looked the same.

'In the four days I didn't shower once,' Schembri said. 'It was horrifying. All the women's jails were full, so we were kept there until they could find us a cell in the system. This was just a remand holding cell. And it was terrifying because nobody knew I was there. My family was trying to call to find out where I was, and nobody could tell them because I wasn't officially in the Corrective Service's system yet. And we weren't allowed to make phone calls or contact anybody.

'For all they knew I could have been dead.'

The officer walked into the cell and shouted her name.

'Schembri, Victoria?' he asked. 'Schembri, time to go.'

Thank goodness. The nightmare was over.

But it wasn't. Oh no, it hadn't even begun.

Schembri was taken and put on a prison truck. She was transported to a place called Mulawa, a prison in Sydney's south-west that you will become very familiar with.

Soon she was squatting naked, a butch prison guard looking up her bum.

'Oh yeah,' she said. 'I got the lot. I was stripped and searched. I had to squat down on the ground completely naked, so if I had put anything up there then it would fall out.'

They checked every inch of her body – first for jewellery, and then for sores.

'All your jewellery is removed,' she said. 'You can't have

anything on. There can be no body rings, studs, nothing. They say that they can be used as a weapon. Apparently girls would try to scratch their veins out with anything sharp.

'And then they checked me for track marks to see if I was a druggie. They also looked for sores, which is another indicator of being a drug abuser. I was what was called a "clean-skin". I had never been in jail before, and I didn't drink, smoke or do drugs. It was like slow motion for me, and surreal to have people studying my arms searching for track marks and drug-induced sores.'

After her medical – an unusually quick one for this place – Mulawa's newest inmate was given a bag of new clothes. Green was the new black . . .

'I was given a tracksuit, a jumper and shorts,' Schembri said. 'And it was all green. All the prison stuff was green, and the only stuff in there that wasn't was the stuff friends or family could give you. That all had to be maroon. I remember thinking it was strange that they didn't give us singlets, but I later found out they had been banned because they were too sexual. Girls would wear them without bras and you could see their boobs.'

In her brand-new green garb, the model, who'd spent her life wearing Versace and Calvin Klein, was frogmarched to her new home – a concrete box with a reinforced steel door – wearing cheap Chinese cotton.

At least it was clean.

The cell door swung open and there was no cellmate lying in wait.

Thank fuck.

There was a bunk, a sink and a toilet.

'I was put into a two-out cell,' Schembri said, referring to a cell that could accommodate only two women. 'And I was lucky because some girls went into four-out and some even to six-out. You don't have any idea who you are going to be put in with, and the odds of landing up with a predator are obviously worse with the more you get in your cell.'

Most attacks – either sexual, violent or both – happen when the steel door is slammed shut.

Sleeping can be deadly in Mulawa.

Schembri walked over to the bottom bunk and unfurled her sheet and blanket. She placed her pillow at the head of the mattress. She was alone, but still terrified.

Are they going to put someone in with me? Oh shit. Who? And what will they to do me?

She laid back on the bed and looked at the tiny perspex window, waiting for a woman's face to fill the peephole before being sent in to join her as her new cellmate.

'I was so scared that all I could do was sit there and rock,' Schembri said. 'I just wanted to shut my eyes and sleep for days.'

But she didn't dare.

Finally, the lock cracked and a woman, clutching blankets of her own, was standing at the door.

Thank goodness.

'This old lady came in,' Schembri said. 'She was a big lady, but old. She looked harmless.'

Schembri introduced herself and then offered the woman the bottom bed.

'I looked at her and thought, *I can't expect you to climb up to the top.* I wasn't afraid of her. She wasn't a career criminal, and she was there for something pathetic, like driving offences. We sat and talked for most of the night, and it turned out we were both as nervous as the other. I mean, it wasn't *brilliant*. She snored the whole night and I didn't sleep a bit, but it could have been a lot worse.'

And soon it was.

'It hit me the next morning. Hard.'

The abuse began with a verbal blasting. Shouts and orders.

'*Get up, you bitches! Get your arses to muster! Rise and shine!*' the no-nonsense guards screamed and barked.

'I was lost from the moment I woke up,' Schembri recalled. 'I had people screaming orders at me and other girls were going off their heads. It was quite brutal and something so foreign to me. I had never been shouted at like that. Never been ordered around like that.'

Dazed, confused and scared, the most glamorous inmate in Mulawa – still stunning despite the green garb and her sleepless night – walked out into the yard for the morning headcount. And that was when the nightmare became real.

She turned after feeling something, or somebody, touch her hair.

'Oh, that's beautiful,' said a beefy inmate as she stroked the back of Schembri's head. 'Such lovely hair. How do you get it so shiny?'

Another lady was soon in her face – an Aboriginal woman this time, her arms covered in sores.

'Aren't you pretty,' she said as she ran her finger across her cheek. 'You're gorgeous. Your skin is so soft. You are going to be popular in here.'

Schembri froze. She said nothing and did nothing as the two women continued to touch her and cover her in compliments.

'As soon as I got there I had women coming up and touching me,' Schembri said. 'It was terrifying and it didn't stop. It was all types of women who were doing it. There were Aboriginal girls, white girls, butch girls and pretty girls coming up to feel me.'

Should I grin and bear it? Will it stop if I ignore it? Or will it be an invitation for something more?

'I was horrified,' Schembri continued. 'I have been in plenty of situations in my life, but nothing like this. I used to be a dancer and I did plenty of double shows, but that was pure show. This was real. This was in-your-face with people I would never associate with. I had never seen somebody covered from head to toe in track marks. Covered in sores from where they have picked their skin because of ice addiction. Nothing like this.'

Maybe I should hit the biggest one? Will that make them stop? Or will I end up with a knife in my back?

They stopped with the compliments and started asking questions.

'You like drugs, pretty girl?' one fired from outside the hungry pack. 'What do you take? Sleepers? Valium? Or are you into the real shit?'

Schembri didn't answer.

'We were in line and there were now five girls standing around me,' Schembri said. 'They kept touching me and asking me about drugs. They were looking me over for track marks. One of them was touching my arm saying, "You're so perfect, you don't even have a needle mark." They were literally clawing over me. A man would never do that – just walk up to you and start running his fingers through your hair and then touching your face. It was like I was a doll.'

Still, she remained silent.

'I was screaming at myself on the inside, but I couldn't get a word out,' Schembri said. 'I was frozen with fear. I was too afraid to do anything. I remember shouting at myself, *What the fuck are you letting them do this for? Get these chicks off you. If this was a guy, you would fucking punch his head in.* I was telling myself to move, to get away, but I was frozen.'

The compliments became veiled invitations.

'There were lots of innuendo,' Schembri said. 'They started telling me that I could get looked after real easy in there if I got myself the right woman.'

Soon the invitations were threats.

'I was offered protection,' Schembri continued. 'They said they would look after me as long as I was willing to fuck them. But there was no way I was doing that. I made a decision right there and then that I would rather be bashed than degrade myself like that.'

And she would be bashed . . . at least four times over the next year.

Later that day, Schembri was allowed to use the phone.

'I'll never forget my first phone call,' she said. 'It was to my partner.' She burst into tears while recounting the conversation. 'I told him that I wouldn't last 12 months in here. I pleaded with him to get me out.'

But only time would get her out. She was a prisoner in one of Australia's worst women's jails.

So what goes on behind the walls of a place like Mulawa?

Let's start with the sex . . .

2

PRISON SEX

Don't Touch Dat!

The silence was shattered as the guard suddenly cracked the lock, swung the door and exploded into the cell. There was no knock, no announcement. Not this time . . .

'No, it was a raid,' said the current prison officer. 'We usually give them plenty of warning before going into their cells. Male guards have to give them some notice so they have a chance to get decent.'

But there was no warning on this freezing morning when two officers, in a bid to capture contraband, launched into the cell for a surprise pre-dawn raid at Sydney's Dillwynia Correctional Centre. Dillwynia is a medium-security facility located in the John Morony Correctional Complex near Windsor, and it houses 260 female inmates.

'This is a search!' screamed one of the officers, now standing in the cell.

The bed turned into a behemoth jack-in-the-box, a woman springing from the blankets after the shock snapped her upright.

'What?' she said. 'What? What is this?'

The guard looked down at the woman, whose eyes finally found focus after being hit with a heavy fluorescent blast.

'Do you have any contraband?' the guard demanded.

The woman slowly shook her head.

'No, boss,' she said softly. 'Nothing to see in here.'

The officer nodded his head. *Yep, she's probably right.* Still, he was going to up-end her cell. He was going to search through every nook and cranny. That was his job.

'She was a little Asian woman,' recalled the officer. 'And I remember how sweet she looked. How innocent. She seemed absolutely harmless, and I was pretty sure we were wasting our time by searching her cell. You find all sorts of things in women's cells: weapons, drugs, phones. But I didn't think this woman was the type to be hiding anything.'

He began rifling through her drawers, the first containing make-up. He pushed at nail polish vials, prodded compacts and thumbed through a rainbow row of lipsticks.

'What do we have here?' shouted the other guard, half his body under the inmate's bed. He slowly eased his way out, dragging a piece of metal with him. He stood up and looked at his find: a thick, hard, round piece of tube.

Surely a weapon, right?

'Yep, that's what we thought,' said the guard, who stopped sifting through the make-up to study the object in his colleague's hand.

'It looked like it could do a lot of damage. You could easily crack a skull with it,' said the officer, remembering what happened that day.

Like a pensioner when their last number drops – 'Bingo!' – the officer beamed. He proudly twisted the *weapon* in his hand, carefully rubbing the metal in his palms.

The lady, who had been silent and completely unconcerned during the search, suddenly spoke. 'Chief, don't touch dat,' she said in a thick Vietnamese accent.

The guard swung around and looked the lady firmly in the face. 'Excuse me?' he demanded. 'You don't tell me what I can and can't touch in here. I will touch whatever I like, whenever I like.'

The meek woman had become brave. 'No, chief,' she said with force. 'You don't understand. Don't touch dat one. Pease.'

The guard tapped the piece of steel against his open palm – first softly, then harder, and harder again. 'Shut up. We've found this weapon. And we will now look for more.'

The woman refused to stay quiet now, despite the apparent threat of being slapped by steel.

'No!' She was pleading. 'No. It not weapon. Pease put down. It not good to touch.'

But the guard wasn't backing down. 'You're in big trouble now,' he shouted. 'Who were you planning on hitting with this? Who were you going to attack?'

The woman blushed a deep shade of red. 'It not weapon,' she said. 'It my dildo. I just attack myself wit it.'

Clang!

The piece of metal bounced off the cell's floor, the guard hurling the weapon-turned-sex toy across the room.

'He almost threw up,' recalled the other guard. 'Seriously, he went green straightaway. I just started pissing myself, laughing hysterically. He was yelling, "*Disgusting, fucking disgusting*", as the giant dildo rolled along the floor.

'And it was a giant. Seriously, it was the size of a baseball bat. And the woman . . . well, she was mortified. She was so embarrassed. She didn't want to tell us what it was but she left us with no choice. She would have been charged with being in possession of a weapon.'

Giant dildos? Yep. They can be found in most cells.

'Some of these girls are in there for a long time,' said the guard. 'And, like everyone, they have their needs. But unfortunately this one had to be confiscated because of its size – it could also be used as a weapon.'

Still green but no longer gagging, the officer reached into a pouch strapped to his bulging belt. He pulled out a pair of white latex gloves.

'Can I have yours too?' he asked his fellow guard, still laughing, and now laughing some more.

Phone Sex

The woman slowly shuffled her way towards the bench.

'Here?' she asked, pointing at the cheap laminate benchtop.

The prison officer said nothing as he pulled the door shut. Nor did he speak as he locked the door.

'Yep,' he said eventually, wrestling the heavy chain of clanking keys. 'That will do.'

He pushed against the door, a hard shove to make sure no one was getting in or, for that matter, out.

'Well,' he demanded, his arms raised in frustration. 'What are you waiting for? Get your gear off.'

The young inmate, new to this Sydney jail, obliged. She quickly ripped off her singlet and dropped it on the floor.

Let's get this over with. Better hurry.

The guard looked at her ample breasts, her nipples already hard.

'Not from him,' the former prisoner revealed. 'It was fucking cold. He was a big, fat slob. Disgusting.'

She then took off her pants, removing her underwear with a singular southbound swoop. Now stark naked, she walked towards the officer slowly, leaning in to give him a kiss.

'The bastard pushed me away,' she recalled. 'He swore at me and said, "Bitch, lean over the bench."'

She followed the order, spreading her palms lightly on the benchtop.

I hope this is quick.

She heard him fumbling with his belt buckle.

Tink! Tink!

And then she felt him enter – small but as hard as the steel door that was stopping anyone from intruding – taking his full weight. It was over in a minute.

Thank God.

Once again the guard was fumbling his belt buckle, this time latching it.

'You'll get your bag by the end of the week,' he said, opening the door. 'As long as you keep your mouth shut.'

'I used to fuck the guards for gear,' said the woman, no longer an inmate, in what would be to most an utterly startling revelation. 'Mostly I would get *pot*, but sometimes it would be *goie* [methamphetamine]. It might sound like it was a bad deal, but for me it was nothing. I was a street girl before I went in. I used to fuck blokes for drugs outside, so really there was no difference.

'It wasn't rape or anything like that. The guards would just approach anyone they fancied and let them know that they could get them things. Anyone who wasn't a butch had something going on. It was the easiest way to get stuff. All the working girls thought nothing of it. It was nothing we hadn't done before.'

Yep, according to former inmates, consensual sex between officers – both female and male – and inmates was rife. Veteran inmate turned activist Kat Armstrong went on the record to expose the sickening sex-swap epidemic in 2013.

'Some women do it willingly,' said the head of the Women in Prison Advocacy Network. 'Because the officer will then bring her special treats – make-up and perfume. It can be the simplest of things. It's a reality and it is going to happen because of the power imbalances that occur with vulnerable women. Some even because they've been prostitutes and that's how they've supported their drug addiction. It becomes another means for them to actually get benefits and favours.'

Blanche Hampton, an ex-Mulawa prisoner, made the astonishing claim that some women would even trade sex for a phone call.

'The rules [in female] prisons are absolutely unbelievable,' Hampton said. 'Look at the consequence of the rule that says you're not allowed to have a phone card. If a woman gets word that her kid is sick and she has used up her phone calls for the week, she panics. The social workers may have gone home and she's desperate. So an officer may offer her an extra phone call for a price. Sex for a 40-cent phone call.'

A current guard laughed off claims of 'widespread sex swapping'.

'Look, it does happen, and we know it happens,' he said. 'Officers have been charged with sexual assault and jailed for it. So of course it sometimes happens consensually. But seriously, it's a blip on the radar. You're kidding yourself if you think the guards go to work and root girls all night.

'The majority of these girls are just putrid. There are no supermodels in jail. Most have no teeth and are disgusting. Sure, you do get the odd glamour that comes through, but she would only make up one per cent of the population. We are talking big butch bitches that would rip you apart, or fucked-up junkies with every disease known to man. You don't want to have to push most of these girls into a cell, let alone fuck them. They are the bottom rung of society.

And there are cameras everywhere. Chances are you would get caught. But most of us are good humans who wouldn't consider stuff like that anyway. You'd have to be pretty sick in the head to go down that path, and most of the men I work with are good people.'

He even suggested that some of the women intimidated male guards by way of sexual advance.

'You would get them propositioning you,' he said. 'And it could be very uncomfortable. Belinda Van Krevel [jailed for two years for stabbing her partner] was notorious for it. When the squad did raids, she would stand at the front of her cell wearing nothing but her undies and bra. The whole time she would play with us. She was a real manipulative bitch.

'She wasn't a bad sort, either. She was tall, brunette and pretty good-looking. She used her looks and body to manipulate people.'

The officer recalled one such moment.

'We went in with a female officer – we had to by law,' he said. 'And she just ignored the woman and concentrated on us. She started talking to one of the male officers. She put her thumb in her mouth and started sucking it. Then she started playing with herself. I mean, what can you do aside from telling her to stop? It's pretty hard to get your job done with that going on. She was always good at manipulating the guards.'

Head to Toe

'Male in the wing,' the male officer shouted, his beefy voice bouncing off the walls of the Mulawa wing. Then again, this time louder, just to make sure. 'Male in the wing! Man coming through!'

Then he banged on the still unopened door – the only one firmly shut.

'Come on,' he said as he rattled his keys. 'You should be at muster. Everyone else is up. This ain't no motel.'

The lock sprang back and he heaved open the heavy door.

He powered his way through. And then he froze.

'Aww shit!' he said, throwing his hands into the air. Then he shrugged. 'Right-o. I'll give you a couple of minutes.'

Face bright red, he turned, walked out and slowly swung the door shut.

'You would often go in and catch them head-to-toe,' said the veteran of NSW women's jails. 'It was very common in every two-out cell. They would be head-to-toe, if you know what I mean.'

Head-to-toe? Well, if you don't know what he means let's clear it up, delicately of course. These two muster no-shows sharing the Mulawa cell were engaged in simultaneous oral sex. Think of a number beginning with 'six' and ending with 'nine'. Right. Got the idea?

The officer had walked in on many girls who liked these particular two numbers, hundreds of times over the years. Still, he was shocked every time he saw a couple going at it 'head-to-toe'.

'As a male you would just have to try to ignore it and be like, "Okay, whenever you finish, girls",' the officer said. 'You would continue around them, and they would only stop when you demanded they come to muster. It's very hard to get that mental image out of your head, no matter how many times you happen to see it.'

We have all heard the stories about sex in men's jails. Most times it is forced upon a younger inmate who lacks the capacity to defend himself against the hardened jailhouse predators. Some men even conduct male-on-male sexual relationships willingly, despite claiming to be heterosexual. The practice is called 'prison sex', and is accepted in prison to be a non-homosexual practice.

A recent report conducted by the University of New South Wales suggests that only seven per cent of male inmates admit to having sex in prison. You could at least double that lean figure for a more honest account, given that most inmates would be reluctant to admit to having sex with another man.

But how about women? What do they get up to in jail? Well, according to a 2011 survey, which saw more than 2000 prisoners take part, more than a third of women in NSW jails have had consensual sex with a fellow inmate. 'Female prisoners were much more sexually active than men,' the study said.

'Thirty-six per cent reported sex with other inmates, while oral sex was involved in about 60 per cent of the encounters.'

The veteran officer claims the survey severely understates the number of women in jail who are sexually active with each other.

'Most of the women in Mulawa had sex,' the officer continued. 'The whole lot, I would say. The ones who didn't want to were forced to. If a new female came in, especially an attractive one, they would be on her in a second. They would tell her to do [a sexual act], and if she didn't then they would force her. One of the girls might just push her down, grab her head and shove it into her crotch. 'Right . . . start licking it,' she would say.

'It was very violent and very common. A rare few in there are doing life sentences, and they will do anything and everything to get what they want. The girls know that and fear that will be used against them. But for the most part it was consensual. It is far more widely accepted in female jails than in male ones. There is no real stigma attached to it. No one is frowned down at for doing it.'

A former Mulawa inmate confirmed that sex was common in the Western Sydney jail.

'Lots of the girls had partners,' she said. 'It was very common and not a secret. Personally, yes, I was hit on. A few times and especially in the 80s when I was younger, more attractive. But I wouldn't say that I was preyed upon. I can't say that I was targeted or saw a lot of that sort of thing going on.'

The Australian Institute of Criminology (AIC) is another organisation to document widespread lesbian relation-ships in prison. The following is from an AIC report called 'Women and Crime: Imprisonment Issues'.

Walking around the NSW and Victorian prisons, it is common to see women holding hands, cuddling on the grass and patting each other's bottoms while walking.

Most prison officers appeared to accept that lesbian relationships are commonplace and noted that when awakening the inmates in a cottage, they frequently encountered couples sleeping together.

Although those women engage in lesbian behaviour, they do not seem to be a direct threat to those who do not, the indirect consequences for the latter lie in the informal inmate stratification system, which may translate into romantic rivalry and subsequent fights.

Such struggles exacerbate the normal degree of tension, which can contribute to the heterosexual first-timer's feeling of stress, unreality and general malaise.

One such prisoner said that, although she had not experienced physical or sexual abuse while on remand, she had witnessed another girl's brutal rape. She believed she could not intervene or tell anyone.

Reportedly drug users, lesbians and recidivists are perceived as a threat to any inmate power groups or hierarchy and are, next to dobbing, the most frequent source of intra-inmate hostility.'

More Dildos

'Miss, can we have some more seeds?' said the green-thumb gardener, wearing, well, green of course . . .

The officer, ready and willing to entertain the inmates who were engaged in something other than drug-taking, fighting or fucking for a change, looked back and smiled.

'Sure,' she said. 'I'll see what I can do. What are you after?'

The inmate met the screw with awkward silence.

'Speak up, sweetie,' the officer said. 'What seeds do you want? Spit it out, hon.'

The young lady, in for aggravated assault, went a shade of red.

'Ummmm,' she paused, before finally blurting it out. 'Zucchini seeds. We need more zucchinis. Or cucumbers if you are out of zucchinis.'

The officer shrugged. 'I'm sure we have zucchinis,' she said. 'They growing good?'

The inmate smiled. 'Yep. Girl's love 'em. We are getting some big ones.'

And they were. And they did.

'We used to have a garden out in minimum-security,' explained a female officer who worked at Bathurst Correctional Centre in the late 80s and is still in the Department of Corrective Services. 'And they would grow vegetables there. The most popular vegetable was the zucchini. I had no idea at first. But that's all they wanted to grow.'

And grow they did, a whole vegetable patch full of zucchinis – *big, hard and long.*

'We had no idea for at least a year,' the officer continued. 'And then someone asked somebody else in the kitchen about the zucchinis.'

So what about the prized zucchinis? The girls love 'em. That's all they grow in the garden.

'The cook said, "Zucchinis?" He had never cooked one in his life. And we were like, "What the . . . oh, yeah".'

And then the cell searches started.

'Yep,' the officer said. 'We found the zucchinis. They were hidden under beds, kept in draws and tucked behind picture frames.'

The big ones anyway.

'Oh, they were quite the item,' the officer explained. 'Most girls couldn't wait and picked them before they were ripe. Only a few got to really mature, and those ones . . . well, they were in huge demand.' In fact, the big ones could be rented out. 'They would put them into plastic gloves so they could share them around. They became currency.'

The unnamed officer has seen more makeshift dildos than she has shivs.

'They are very creative with their dildos,' the officer continued. 'Men spend time on shivs, but girls will be [using their creativity] for sexual gratification rather than protection or violence. They use bottles, whatever they can. The zucchini was probably the oddest I've seen. Not because of the vegetable itself, but because they would share it. The filth that comes with that sort of thing, they just don't care. I reckon about 90 per cent of them are junkies, and they just don't give a fuck about hygiene.'

No, that's not right . . . I was told of the *cleanest* dildo ever.

'I saw some dildos in there,' said four-year Mulawa inmate Victoria Schembri.

'But the most common was the old "Dynamo". They'd get the plastic gloves that were given out, and they would open them up and fill them with laundry powder. Yeah, they would fill it up with Cold Power or Dynamo or whatever was going around, and they would make it whatever size they liked – that's why it was so popular. They could make it small, big or bigger – whatever was comfy and got them off – and then they would tie it off and use it as a dildo.'

Wolf Whistles and Haircuts

Victoria Schembri, the former model and entertainer turned felon, walked into her new home: a sterile wing in the infamously rough Dillwynia women's jail in western Sydney. She had survived her three-month stretch in Mulawa. Sure, there had been plenty of hair touching and everyday innuendo – even a slap or two on the bum – but that was as far as the sexual harassment went. She had managed to remain almost anonymous. But that was all about to change.

'I saw someone I knew as soon as I walked in,' Schembri said. 'And she was a lady with a very big mouth.'

So. A big mouth?

'Oh, she knew my history,' Schembri said. 'She knew everything about me. She knew that I was a *Penthouse* pet. She knew that I had worked in TV and film. She even knew that I had had an offer for another *Penthouse* centrefold shoot just before I went in.'

And Schembri knew that this woman was going to tell every other woman in the wing about her past.

'That would make her a target,' explained a current Dillwynia guard. 'A big target. People with a name, infamous people or celebrities become targets as soon as they get in.

They all read the papers in prison. They also watch the TV and listen to the radio. They will latch onto anything they can and use it against that person.'

And that is exactly what they did to Dillwynia's new beauty queen.

'Next thing, everyone knew exactly who I was and what I used to do,' Schembri said. 'They knew I used to be a cover girl and a centrefold. They also found out I was a *Penthouse* model and that I had done some TV. And that was it – that's when it kicked off.'

Hey, Elle Macpherson . . . how about a fuck? I'll fuck you like no man has ever fucked you. Come on over here and get the good stuff.

'They didn't let up,' Schembri said. 'There were constant wolf whistles wherever I would walk. I would go running and they would follow me, telling me what they would like to do to me at night. I had three or four girls surround me in the yard and just start touching me. To be honest, I was terrified. But I was numb. I just froze when they did it and hoped it would go away. Thank fuck I had my own room in a group house.'

Still, things were equally terrifying in the four-out house in the infamous jail.

'I was living with three murderers,' Schembri said. 'One of the girls was Kathy *Yeo*. She had chopped her partner's head off.'

That's right, our model inmate was placed in a house with the psychiatric nurse who had been sentenced to serve 28 years after being found guilty in 1997 of shooting her lover Christopher Dorrian – a patient with whom she had had daily sex with in a hospital storeroom. She subsequently decapitated Dorrian, placed his head in a sports bag and threw it into the Cooks River in Sydney's Inner West.

'Yeah, she wasn't the only killer in my house,' said Schembri. 'I was also locked up with another husband killer, a girl name Danielle Stewart.'

Stewart was jailed for four years after being found guilty of manslaughter. The bubbly blonde had stabbed her husband, Chaim Kimel, in a drunken rage in 2008. The then 32-year-old had picked up an antique knife and plunged it into her 'dominating' husband in a grisly Eastern Suburbs domestic attack.

Stewart's sentencing judge revealed the woman had a history of drug and alcohol abuse, anorexia and self-harm. She had also been sexually abused by three different people and suffered trauma relating to her mother's cancer death.

'Yep, we had them all in that house,' Schembri continued. 'Another woman in there had had someone offed, so of the four of us in there, I was the only one who hadn't murdered anyone. Bloody hell, they were killers and I was in there for being a victim of domestic violence!'

But her very own house of horrors – the black widows' nest – was nothing compared to the jail jungle outside her front door. The first predator disguised herself as a friend.

'An Indian girl called Sami was in the very next cell to me,' Schembri recalled. 'I used to get up real early and sit out the front of my cell. She was a really good cook. She cooked some amazing Indian food. I remember her being exceptionally nice – very chatty – and would give me some of the food she'd cooked.'

Schembri thought nothing of the food offerings. But then the gifts got weird.

'She would ask me if I liked socks,' Schembri said. 'She would tell me she would be able to get me good socks.'

What the fuck? What do I want your socks for? I have my own socks.

'Anyway, I figured she just liked socks,' Schembri said. And she was right. 'And then a pair of socks came in. They were a gift from my husband, and they were these big rainbow socks. She had her eye on them and kept telling me how much she liked them. I wasn't even allowed to have them because they were the wrong colour.'

So Schembri gave Sami the socks.

'The next thing I know she is cooking for me all the time,' Schembri said. 'Then she's following me around, wanting to play cards. Then she's grabbing me on the arse and putting the hard word on me. She had been grooming me all along and expected me to be her girlfriend. It was fucking wrong and got pretty nasty.'

But not as nasty as the visits room and it's full-frontal filth.

'How's school?' Schembri asked. 'Are you being a good girl?'

The young girl looked back at her mum, who was dressed in prison green, shockingly skinny but still smiling.

'Yeah, it's okay,' she said. 'How about you? What do you do in here?'

Schembri gritted her teeth and lied. 'You know what? It's not too bad. Not too bad at all. We have plenty of things to do. I get to exercise a lot. I run every day. I watch TV and listen to the radio too. I even have a job. It's not too much different from being at home, except for the fact that I don't get to see you. And that's really the only thing that sucks. And it sucks big-time.'

She leaned over and planted a kiss on her child. Schembri then looked at her other daughter, the youngest of her three.

'What's wrong, sweetie?' she asked.

The little girl had been stone-cold silent and completely distracted. She was looking around the room, studying the sad scene – women crying as they talked to their parents, mums holding their babies, and another woman . . . well, the young girl didn't know exactly what the woman on the next table was doing. Or, more to the point, what the man she was visiting was doing to *her*.

Is he hurting her? Why doesn't she ask for help?

Schembri followed her daughter's gaze. '*Aaaah!*' she shouted. 'Don't look at that, hon! Quick. Look at me. Right here. Look at my face. That's it . . . Here I am.'

With her daughter firmly focused on her, Schembri stood up.

'Officer!' she demanded. 'Officer, over here.'

A guard, one of only two watching the almost 30 women assembled in the visits section, some with as many as five visitors, walked towards the table where Schembri was sitting with her husband and three children.

Schembri turned to her left and growled at the now groaning woman.

'There are fucking kids right here,' she hissed. 'You're sick. How could you? They will be scarred for life. They don't have to see that. They should *never* have to see that.'

The woman refused to acknowledge the disgusted mother, and continued to moan, even louder.

'The girl next to me was getting fingered in the visit,' Schembri said. 'I was sitting there with my kids, and she was carrying on while her partner was getting stuck into her. Jesus! How do you explain that to your kids? They looked at me and innocently asked, "Mum, what's that man doing to that woman?" It was right in your face.'

The officer reached Schembri's table and looked down at her and her family.

'Would you like to move?' the officer asked. 'I can put you on a table over there.'

Yep. The officer didn't stop the fingers, the full-frontal filth. Apparently it was easier to move Schembri and her four guests, leaving the stammering young mother to explain what had happened to her scared, shocked and stunned kids.

According to a current corrections officer, the above is true. The veteran guard has seen fingers and fists find their way into prisoners' pants. She has seen women jerk men off – suck them off, too. She has seen even more, but we will get to that a little later.

'It still happens everywhere today,' she said. 'And it is very difficult to stop.'

Really? In a fully supervised prison visit? In front of trained guards?

'Look, they just get very close during the visit,' she said. 'They will sit there holding hands. They will be talking close. Then a hand will go on a leg. Soon they will be kissing. And then, well, a hand will slip down the pants and they are into it.

'Back in the 80s and early 90s it was very easy. The girls didn't wear overalls, so it was quite simple for their partners to slip a hand in. It's a bit harder now, but it still happens. It happens a lot. They just cut out their pockets and away they go.'

And if she isn't wearing prison-altered, 'easy access' overalls, well, she can always pull his pants off.

'You see that as much as you see them getting fingered,' the officer continued. 'If not more. They will just go over into the corner and start jerking [the men] off. They have no shame. They even get down on their knees and give head-jobs.'

Again . . . Really? In a prison? How? Why don't you just stop them?

'Look, you only have two officers in a room: one up the front and one up the back,' the officer continued. 'But there would be 30 or 40 prisoners in the visit, so it would be very hard to watch everything. We would be more focused on looking for drugs – that's what the bosses want us to stop and what you can get a charge for. Sex? Fingering? Well, that isn't going to end up in court. Sure, we're told to stop it if we see it, but we can't watch out for everything. We have to prioritise when there are only two guards covering a room full of people.'

41

But surely you can pull them up on it? Pull them up when they are pulling each other off?

'Of course we stop them if we see it,' the officer continued. 'We don't want to see that going on. It's completely disgusting. There are kids in the room, and we certainly want to protect them. No kid should ever have to see that.

'And it isn't just kids. You've got people coming in who've never experienced anything like that. Law-abiding parents come in to see their daughters and they are subjected to full-on sex. Brothers and sisters, maybe accountants and nurses – they come in too and watch a filthy animal getting fingered. It's horrifying for the respectable families who come in to see their relatives.'

But the inmates don't give a shit.

'The're just shameless,' the officer continued. 'They couldn't care less who they do it in front of. They would do it in front of the Pope if he was unlucky enough to be in there visiting someone.'

And what do they do when they get busted?

'They just tell you to nick off,' the officer said. 'You ask them to separate and they give you a look like they've done nothing wrong.'

Yeah? What's the big deal? I only get to see her once a month. Nick off, bitch.

'It's just crazy how they behave,' the officer added. 'They have no respect for anyone, especially us.'

*

The guard could go home; Schembri couldn't.

'I was hit with that sort of shit every day,' the model inmate said. 'I saw things that will never leave me. Watching two people have sex is not normal, but that's what I saw every day.'

Schembri first walked in on two women having sex while in remand.

Whoops. Sorry.

'It was in the showers,' she said. 'At the back of Silver-water [Correctional Complex]. I walked in and the shower door was open. I went to use the shower and, *fuck me*, there were two women at each other. They were just all over each other. It was gross.'

The first time would not be the last.

'Girls were getting it on all the time,' Schembri said. 'Two girls in my house became partners. They would go into the bedroom as soon as we got back to the house and they would go at it. You could hear them whenever they were having sex because they were ridiculously loud.

'One time I walked into a friend's house at [minimum-security] Emu Plains [Correctional Centre]. A girl invited me in for a cuppa, and I walked in and there were two girls on the table having a 69. They stopped as soon as they saw me. "Oh fuck, sorry," one of them said. And like that they went off to the bedroom and continued where they left off.'

Schembri said sex was as good as money in jail.

'They worked out I could cut hair,' said the former inmate. 'So I started cutting their hair. One woman said she didn't have any money, but she could give me a blowie if I liked? I just said, "I'm all good." She was a tough chick, and

I said look out for me in return. Sex was tradable. It was just currency.'

The officer again agreed with the inmate.

'Heaps do it,' she confirmed. 'They all have sex and use it to get whatever they want. It's just the norm.'

But what she didn't agree with was the low-ball figure that a third of women inmates have had consensual sex with someone else in jail.

'Nah,' she said. 'That's wrong. I would go more with 80 per cent. I remember walking in on them all the time. They would be top-to-tail, and they wouldn't even acknowledge you. They would just be "Hey, miss" and go back to what they were doing. It was no big deal. I think that's just how they survive.

'And most of them weren't gay. Sure, you would get the odd person who was gay, but the percentage in jail would reflect society – it wouldn't be any higher. So there were a lot of people involved in lesbian behaviour who would not be on the outside. It was consensual in that they didn't make complaints and let it happen, but some people must have been intimidated into it. I'm sure some felt pressured and others did it to survive.'

And it's not hard to see who is pressuring whom, according to the officer at least.

'They get in there and all of a sudden one becomes the male and the other becomes the female,' she said. 'You can tell who is who. It's a quite dominant/submissive relationship.'

And oftentimes the female inmates love sex so much that they return to prison for another fling . . .

A Table, a Chair, and then a Child

The officer tapped her feet to the irresistible sound of rock-and-roll – guitars blasting, drums belting. The band was at full tilt, their Fenders and Marshalls making a wall of sound as high and as thick as any of the sandstone ones surrounding the historic Bathurst Jail.

'They're good!' screamed the female officer to the inmate standing beside her, his head bouncing to the beat.

'They sure are,' he said. 'This is awesome. This is the best family day ever!'

The band continued with hit after hit, covers not originals – not that anybody cared – as children played with clowns while eating fairy floss. There was also a pony and plenty of food.

All were entertained, especially the two under the table.

'Quick!' screamed the male prison officer – the short, sharp, urgent shrill suddenly snapping the officer from her rock-and-roll rhythm. 'Over there. Look!'

What the fuck? What are they doing? Nah. They couldn't be – not at a family day.

The officer ran immediately towards the plastic tables and chairs that had been brought in to create a temporary eatery. She went as fast as she could, honing in on the seemingly vacant table with the chairs pushed out of the way.

She looked down at the inmate, who had his pants down and was pounding away.

'Get up!' she screamed. 'What do you think you're doing? For Christ's sake, there are kids everywhere!'

The inmate rolled off his woman, cock pointing straight towards the sky as he addressed the officer from the concrete floor of the yard.

'No problem,' he said. 'All done here. It's been a while, if you know what I mean.'

She wanted to kick him straight in his dick.

Filthy animal.

Michael Caldwell stood and pulled up his pants, much the same as he did six years earlier, in 1982, when he killed Peter Parkes and Constantine Giannaris separately after they had paid him for sex. Caldwell was serving life for the brutal murders.

Giannaris, the Greek consul general to Australia, was found dead on 16 November 1982, while Peter Parkes, a gay activist and schoolteacher, was murdered on 20 October. Both men were found gagged and tied, and had been involved in sex shortly before their deaths.

Caldwell and a 16-year-old co-offender known only as 'MT' were arrested and convicted of the stabbing murders after stolen jewellery recovered from a pawnshop linked them to the shocking crimes dubbed the 'Gay Blade Killings'.

And now, just six years later at Bathurst Jail, Caldwell was once again having sex.

'There was a female prisoner who had recently been released,' said a former Bathurst officer. 'She was what we would call a "high-maintenance prisoner" – we all knew her. Anyway, after her sentence she kept on coming back to visit this lifer named Caldwell. He was in there for a couple of gay-bashing murders. It was quite strange that she was coming in to visit him, because he was never getting out.

'They apparently became friends while in jail, and that continued after she got out. They maintained their friendship by writing letters and with her visiting him.'

Then came the family day ... the loud bands, knocked-over chairs and disgusting grunts and groans.

'We had [family days] back in the 80s,' the officer continued. 'They were a bit like a gala day, and they would happen every three or so months. It was a smooth-over thing to help build relationships, and we would have barbecues and that sort of thing. I actually arranged for bands to come to a couple of them. People would come in from the outside and give talks, and there were a bunch of activities organised for both the cons and their families. It was a way to break the ice between the officers and the prisoners.'

Girlfriends would come in too.

'This particular day she came in for the family day to visit Caldwell,' the officer recalled. 'She was a real big junkie, and we were worried about her bringing stuff in and giving it to him. That was our main concern. But she came in and soon they disappeared.'

Vanished ... but soon found.

'They were having sex under a table,' the officer said. 'They got busted and separated, but it was all done by the time we got to them. They were finished, if you know what I mean.

'We said, "Get up ... What are you doing?" and they replied, "Nothing, nothing." He might have been done in a minute. I mean, he'd been in jail for ages and wouldn't have had sex for who knows how long . . . with a woman anyhow, so it mightn't have taken that long.'

About eight months later Caldwell approached the officer with a bombshell request.

'Miss,' he said. 'Ummm, well, I need to get a day release.'

The officer laughed. 'Day release? You? Yeah, right. You're in here for life. Why would we ever let you out?'

Caldwell looked sheepish. 'I need to get out to be there for the birth of my first child. I'm going to be a dad.'

The officer went white.

Oh shit!

'The woman actually fell pregnant,' the officer said. 'And she claimed that it was his. Anyway, we didn't know whether it was or not, but we did know that they had had sex on that day, and the timeframe was about right. And, yep, he actually applied for permission to go to the birth. The request went all the way to the governor. Caldwell was convinced the child was his. It was a little difficult for him to prove it was his back then and he was denied permission, but I think he would have been denied anyway. It would have been fairly embarrassing for a bloke serving time to go to the birth of his child when he had been locked up for six years. There would have been some explaining to do.'

So what was the attraction?

'He was an average-built guy with that greaser-type hair,' said the officer. 'I suppose he was attractive. He was always clean and tidy. Lifers tended to be quite clean and organised because this was their home and they respected their rooms and themselves. He looked after himself, went to the gym a bit, and he worked. But I don't know why she thought she wanted to have a child with a guy who was never getting out. Who knows what was going on in her head.'

Sex isn't the biggest problem in jail. Naughtiest? Sure. But nothing compared to the drug epidemic.

3

SMACK AND SPEED

Deadly Drug Party

The brown began bubbling on the silver piece of foil, the clump of heroin no match for the flaming BIC lighter. Tracy-Lee Brannigan inserted the end of the syringe into the molten mess as her cellmate, Lauren Ironside, watched on.

Hands shaking, the needle tip bouncing about in the high-grade smack, Brannigan steadied herself before sucking back the plunger on the other end of the syringe.

She held on tightly to the syringe, now fully loaded, as she searched her body for a fully functioning vein.

Left arm? Veins collapsed. Right arm? All collapsed. Legs? All collapsed.

She smiled as she looked at the top of her left hand – bulging blue lines.

Perfect.

The needle hovered over her hand, the woman making sure of her mark, fighting hard against her shakes. Pumping her fist below the makeshift tourniquet, she edged the end of the needle into the rising vein . . . and pushed the plunger.

Needle still stuck to the top of her hand, she slowly slumped down into her prison bed.

Bliss.

But there was no time to rest; this was a prison cell party. Ironside, Brannigan's lesbian lover, had just been given bail. She would be sent to a rehabilitation centre tomorrow. With their cell door locked and the rest of the wing oblivious, the jailbirds stayed up swapping stories, saliva and needles. They also took pills.

Soon enough, the drugs were gone. The used needles went back into the empty shampoo bottle. And they both went to sleep.

Brannigan, a 41-year-old mother of three, would never wake up. Her lover would find her dead, collapsed on the floor, at 4 am.

'I tried to give her mouth-to-mouth,' Ironside said. 'But she was cold and stiff.'

Brannigan's death was front-page news.

'Drugs in Prison,' the papers screamed in bold letters and black ink. 'Mother Dead after Heroin Smuggled into Cell.'

How could there be drugs in prison? Drugs in prison?! This is an outrage!

The general public was shocked. Anyone who had ever been in jail, worked in a jail or had spoken to someone who'd been to a jail wasn't.

Drugs in jail? No shit, Sherlock.

'There have always been drugs in prison, and there always will be drugs in prison,' said a retired corrections officer. 'The easiest way to get it in was to just go and throw a tennis ball containing a bag of drugs over the fence. You would normally know that drugs had come in when the women were going around asking for a pair of cutters. They needed something to get into the tennis ball after the drugs had been placed inside and it had been glued back together. They would say they needed the cutters for something in the nursery, but they would use them to get at the heroin.

'Drugs also came into the jail in nappies. You would have babies coming to visit mum with heroin shoved down their diaper. There are a million ways they got drugs, and it was everywhere.'

But the public pounced and the media stormed following the prison death by drug overdose. Brannigan's heartbroken mother fronted the press and demanded to know how this had happened. *Who* let this happen?

'Any mother that would go through this would have to wonder: how?' Sandra Kelly told the ABC. 'When she first went to jail for [drugs], she came out worse than when she went in. And the longer the stretch, the worse she got.'

Prison activist and former inmate Kat Armstrong – one of the last people to see Brannigan alive – fuelled the flames, dumping a drum of petrol straight onto the NSW Department of Corrective Services.

'It could have been avoided,' Armstrong said, who had visited Brannigan the day before she was found dead in her cell. 'It really could have been. If they'd only just taken notice.'

Armstrong, the long-time head of the Women in Prison Advocacy Network, claimed that her friend was clearly affected by drugs when she'd visited.

The former inmate slammed authorities for locking the 'off her face' prisoner in her cell at 3.30 that afternoon. 'There are policies and procedures for this very reason. From my knowledge, the policy is that if a person is suspected of using drugs or is intoxicated, they are put into what is called a dry cell; that is a cell with absolutely nothing in it. The cell is monitored by cameras 24/7. And it also allows constant medical intervention.'

Armstrong continued: 'The system failed her badly. Yes, obviously she took drugs of her own volition. She was a drug addict struggling hard with addiction. She needed help.'

Sandra Kelly pleaded for action to be taken after her daughter's senseless death in jail. 'I hope someone carries this on and we get some answers. We need to get some help for these girls. That's what Tracy would have wanted.'

And, indeed, someone did 'carry it on': the NSW Coroner.

An inquest into the death of Tracy-Lee Brannigan began on 10 June 2014 at the NSW Coroner's Court. Prison staff, inmates, police, medical staff and experts would all give evidence in the inquest, which had the power to overhaul the Corrections system.

'Tracy-Lee's body was identified by Ms Leanne O'Toole on 25 February 2013,' said NSW Deputy State Coroner Paul MacMahon. 'Ms O'Toole was, at the time, the Acting General Manager of the Dillwynia Correctional Centre and had known Tracy since her arrival at that centre.

'The date of her death is not a matter of contention. Tracy-Lee was observed to be alive when placed in her cell at about 3.30 pm. She was subsequently found deceased at about 5 am on 25 February.

'The cause of Tracy-Lee's death was not contentious. Following her death, an autopsy was performed by Dr Kendall Bailey, a forensic pathologist. Based on her findings at autopsy, and taking into account the toxicology and serology reports she received, Dr Bailey concluded that the cause of death was due to heroin toxicity. It was found that in Tracy-Lee's blood there was a potentially fatal level of morphine and metabolites specific to heroin. I accept Dr Bailey's conclusion as to the cause of Tracy-Lee's death.

'The primary issue for this inquest was to inquire into the manner, or circumstances, of Tracy-Lee's death. There was also the need to investigate the circumstances of her incarceration in order to ensure there were no systematic failures that led to, or contributed to, her death.'

In short, the inquest was called to see whether or not Corrective Services locked Brannigan in her cell for a 17-hour stint, despite knowing that she was heavily affected by drugs and in need of medical help.

'The answer must be that society, having affected the arrest and the incarceration of persons who have seriously breached its laws, owes a duty to those persons, of ensuring their punishment is restricted to loss of liberty, and is not exacerbated by ill-treatment or privation while waiting trial or serving sentences,' said former State Coroner Kevin Waller. 'The rationale is that by making mandatory a full inquiry into deaths in prison and police cells the government provides a positive incentive to custodians to treat prisoners in a humane fashion, and satisfies the community that deaths in such places are properly investigated.'

Allegations had been made that Corrective Services had been negligent in their duty of care by failing to send the inmate for medical assistance after learning she had taken an opiate.

Armstrong claimed that Brannigan was affected by drugs when she visited the woman on the afternoon before her death. She said staff should have intervened, and by doing so would have prevented her death.

'In her evidence [Armstrong] said that there was no doubt in her mind that at the time of the visit Tracy-Lee was seriously affected by drugs,' the Coroner said. 'Specifically, some form of opiate. In addition to the matters she referred to in her statement, in her evidence she said that she had also indirectly raised her concerns with a male corrections officer on her way out after the visit. Once again, she did not directly say that she thought Tracy-Lee was under the influence of drugs but believed her comments to the officer would have implied that was the case.

'Ms Armstrong made a statement to police on 4 March 2013. In that statement she asserted that at the time of her visit she formed the opinion that Tracy-Lee was under the influence of some form of opiate or pill of some sort. She said that she asked her what she had taken, however Tracy-Lee denied that she had taken any drugs. She said that, because of her state, Tracy-Lee was not in a position to contribute very much to their conversation.

'Ms Armstrong said that she did not specifically tell any Corrective Services staff of her concern because she believed that Tracy-Lee's condition was obvious to them. She said that she engaged in some loud conversation with Tracy-Lee that she expected would draw attention to Tracy-Lee's condition. She did not see it as being her role to "dob" on her friend so did not specifically tell any Corrective Services staff of her concerns. Ms Armstrong subsequently repeated her assertion on national television.'

Tracy-Lee's cellmate was also grilled in the very public inquiry.

'Lauren Ironside was Tracy-Lee's cellmate at the time of her death,' the Coroner said. 'Ms Ironside found her deceased and called for assistance on the morning of 25 February 2013. An electronic interview of some 666 questions was conducted with Ms Ironside on 25 February 2013.

'Ms Ironside also gave evidence at the inquest. In her evidence at the inquest Ms Ironside said that at the time of Tracy-Lee's return to the cell, following her visit with Ms Armstrong, she formed the opinion that Tracy-Lee was under the influence of drugs. This suggestion was new evidence and contradicted the statement that she made in her interview on 25 March 2013 at answer 291 when she said that Tracy-Lee, on her return from the visit, was not "stoned".

'The allegations made by Ms Armstrong and Ms Ironside are very serious. If, at the time of her return from her visit with Ms Armstrong, she was under the influence of drugs it would not have been appropriate for her to be locked in the cell for the night. It would have been necessary, in accordance with Corrective Services procedure, for her to be taken to the clinic and examined by a Justice Health nurse and, if it was found that she was so affected, placed in an observation cell until the effects of the drug had dissipated.'

Corrections staff were also put on trial and threatened with discipline.

'If it was the case that Tracy-Lee was so affected, and corrections officers knowingly failed to take her for assessment and observation, it would be necessary for me to consider making recommendations that disciplinary action be commenced against such corrections officers,' the Corner said.

The NSW Coroner interviewed corrections staff and medical officials, and had an expert on drugs review the CCTV footage of Brannigan during her visit with Armstrong in a determined bid to reveal the truth.

'Having examined the CCTV of the visit, Dr Perl was strongly of the opinion that Tracy-Lee was not drug affected at the time of the visit,' the Coroner concluded.

So what really happened? When did Tracy-Lee take the lethal dose of heroin? And who was to blame?

'The only direct evidence available as to what happened after Tracy-Lee and Ms Ironside were locked in at 3.30 pm was what Ms Ironside told the police in her interview on 25 February 2013,' the Coroner continued. 'In summary, she said that Tracy-Lee gave her a Rivotril tablet and after that Ms Ironside went to sleep. Ms Ironside also said that before she fell asleep she also saw Tracy-Lee take some tablets as well. In her statement Ms Ironside said that this occurred after lockdown; however, in her evidence she said that the tablets were consumed prior to lockdown and not afterwards.

'I have already found Ms Ironside's evidence to be questionable. I found that her evidence on this matter is also unsatisfactory. I do not accept that Tracy-Lee consumed Rivotril tablets as asserted when Ms Ironside said she did. In this regard, I had the benefit of the evidence of Dr Judith Perl.

'At autopsy, fresh injection marks were found on her body. There was a great deal of evidence available to suggest that Tracy-Lee continued to use illicit substances whilst in custody and was known for her drug-seeking behaviour. Heroin was her drug of choice. I am satisfied that it is more likely than not that, sometime after she and Ms Ironside were locked in their cell on 24 February 2013, Tracy-Lee administered heroin to herself, and that administration resulted in her death.'

NSW police paint a far clearer picture, describing the death as a lesbian lover's prison drug party gone wrong.

Detective Inspector Gary James told the inquiry that Brannigan had formed a lesbian relationship with several female inmates, including her cellmate, Ironside.

The high-ranking police officer said Ironside supplied the drugs in return for sex.

On the night of Brannigan's death, he said the pair had a 'drug party' in their cell, with heroin and prescription drugs, to celebrate Ironside's bail the following day to a rehabilitation centre.

The autopsy found fresh track marks on Brannigan's left hand, and officers discovered syringes hidden in a shampoo bottle inside her cell.

Former Dillwynia inmate Victoria Schembri, the model inmate whom you have met, confirmed that Brannigan had been in a lesbian relationship with Ironside since the pair met at Emu Plains Jail, on the western side of Sydney, in 2010. Schembri described the pair as 'peas in a pod', who followed each other throughout the NSW Corrective Services system.

'Tracy wasn't one of my favourite people in jail,' Schembri recalled. 'She was a well-known druggie. Lauren was a rough kid, but nice. And Tracy knew exactly what she was doing. She just used her for drugs. It was an every-night occurrence for girls to go into lockdown, take drugs and have sex. And I don't think there was anything special about that night. Lauren and Tracy had been together for a long time. They were together for a couple of years at least.'

Ironside was infatuated with the mother of three from Wollongong, according to Schembri.

'Tracy-Lee used her as a toy,' she said. 'And she was the one with all the power in the relationship. She was just using her for drugs. Lauren was a pretty sweet kid, if you got her by herself. She could get the gear in, and I think she loved Tracy-Lee. That goes on a lot in jail.'

'It was a bit both ways. Lauren knew that Tracy wanted the drugs, but Lauren was willing to do whatever because she wanted Tracy. They were together at Emu Plains before. They used to work their way back to each other by using the system. Tracy was kicked out of Emu Plains and Lauren worked her way over to Dillwynia to be with her. She changed her behaviour to get reclassified.

'Anyway, I don't think you can blame anyone for what happened. They took the drugs and knew the consequences.'

Let's back up a bit . . .

The inmate looked Tracy Brannigan firmly in the eyes. 'I've gotta piss,' she said. 'I'm gunna fucking burst.'

Brannigan laughed and nodded. 'Fuck, hey? Better you piss in the corner than piss in your pants.'

Kat Armstrong smiled, turned and then she squatted. With her prison-issue pants wrapped around her ankles, she let her bladder go, her bright-yellow piss steaming as soon as it hit the blistering steel tray of the prison truck, heated not only by the tropically hot day but also by the diesel exhaust, which ran directly under their windowless cage.

Armstrong moved away, sat down and put her pants back on. 'Fuck, that stinks,' she said, looking at the pool of piss spilling to the front of the tray as the driver hit the brakes. 'Sorry, girls.'

Brannigan looked at her. 'Yep. Good thing is we're only going to be locked in this piss-stinking furnace for another ten hours. We must almost be at Coffs Harbour by now.'

Brannigan and Armstrong burst out laughing, and a 21-year friendship, that would only end because of a drug overdose tragedy, was formed.

This is the uncensored story of Tracy-Lee Brannigan's death as told by Kat Armstrong, the woman who police would accuse of delivering the drugs that killed her best friend.

Armstrong is in tears as she begins, revealing she'd had a fight with her friend just hours before Brannigan died.

'I grabbed her,' Armstrong said. 'I asked her what she had taken. What she was on. I spent my last-ever 20 minutes yelling at her, screaming at her to get her shit together because her parole was coming up. I told her she had to pull back on the drugs because she wouldn't get parole or custody of her five-year-old kid.'

The tears continue as Armstrong recalls her friend's disgust after she attempted to dob her in for doing drugs.

'She looked at me and said, "What the fuck are you doing?" She gave me a death stare and walked off, filthy on me.'

Armstrong had, moments before, tried to alert the posse of prison officers to her friend's drug problem, before the hit that would prove to be fatal.

'I was so worried that I gave her a hug at the end, with all the screws around me, and said loudly, because I wanted them to hear, "Tracy, pull your fucking head in. Please stop doing this." I did it on purpose so they would hear, which in prison is considered a Dog act. But I had to do it because

61

I wanted them to take responsibility for her. I was leaving and I couldn't take care of her. I was so desperate. I would never Dog on a mate, and I never had before and never will again, but I was just so worried.'

Brannigan was furious with Armstrong. She turned and stormed off in a rage, never to see her friend again.

'When I yelled that out, the officers turned around,' Armstrong said. 'And Tracy looked at me with this look of, *Did you really just fucking say that?* She couldn't believe I'd Dogged on her. That was the last time I saw her. The next morning I got a phone call from someone telling me she's dead. It just breaks my heart that we ended things like that.'

Kat and Tracy became friends during that horror transport from Grafton to Sydney. Yep . . . they bonded with their feet hovering over a mobile puddle of piss.

'I first met Tracy in 1993,' Armstrong said. 'We crossed paths in Mulawa, but I can't say we were particularly close. We knew who each other were but we'd never spent any time together.'

But that changed when the two escapees – both women were on the run – were captured in northern New South Wales at about the same time and sent to the infamous Grafton Jail in 1997. Armstrong had dodged bail and was living in Mullumbimby when she was caught. Brannigan was picked up in Nimbin after escaping Emu Plains on a prison tractor, her then lover by her side.

'She had stolen the dairy vehicle and taken up to Nimbin with her partner, a girl named Esther,' Armstrong said. 'She ended up getting caught and came into Grafton, where I was at the time. I had just been classified and was set to go back to Sydney to serve my sentence. She was immediately sent back to Sydney because that is where she had escaped from.'

The horror ride to Sydney became bearable thanks to some jailbird banter.

'We were put into a truck together,' Armstrong said. 'It was a little diesel truck, all steel with no windows. It was horrible. It stank and we could hardly breathe. We were put into it for 13 hours, with one 30-minute stop for a toilet break and a baked bean sandwich. At one stage I was hyperventilating. I passed out on the floor, and the officers didn't even stop to check on me. They had cameras so they could see what was going on in the back, but they didn't care. I was curled up in the fetal position.

'I needed to piss. I turned to the girls and asked them if it was okay. They said, "Do what you have to do." So I went to the corner and did a piss.'

The other girls looked on.

What's the fastest piss you've ever had?

Don't know – maybe 40 seconds.

Ha. Got ya. Try 110 kilometres per hour.

'Esther and her thought it was hilarious,' Armstrong said. 'It gave them an excuse to pass the time by putting shit on me all the way to Sydney. But oh fuck, did it stink. Anyway, it broke the trip up and we ended up having a laugh over the horrendous situation. It made us become good friends.'

The friendship solidified while the pair did time together at Mulawa. And it continued when Armstrong was released from jail and turned her attentions to helping women in prison; her friends were understandably at the top of her list.

'When I got out and got my shit together, I stayed close to her,' Armstrong said. 'I helped her out with her case. I had set up WIPAN [Women in Prison Advocacy Network] by then. I didn't think her solicitor was very good, and I was trying to get her new representation.'

Armstrong went to visit Brannigan on 24 February 2013 – the day before her death – after a request from her friend's husband.

'I went in because her family asked me to,' Armstrong said. 'They were worried about her because she was on a downward spiral. She had parole coming up in a couple of months, and they wanted me to set her straight. Her mother had spoken to her on the phone, and she was really concerned because Tracy sounded like she was off her face. They had been noticing a decline in her health and state of mind. Anyway, I got a call and a family member told me she was on drugs. They told me to get there and talk some sense into her – they had tried and couldn't do anything. They couldn't get through to her and thought I was the only person who could.'

So Armstrong booked her visit. She called the jail and was given an appointment to see Brannigan at 2 pm. She was told she was only allowed to visit for an hour.

What has she been up to? She's in the shit again. She must be on sanctions to only be given an hour.

'The visit was supposed to start at 2 pm but I was still waiting at 2.20 pm,' Armstrong said. 'I knew something was wrong and I kept on going and asking them where she was. They told me they couldn't find her.'

What the fuck? You can't find her? Isn't this a jail? Seriously . . . How do you lose a prisoner?

'She finally comes out – in overalls because she's on sanctions – and I knew as soon as I saw her that she was off her head,' Armstrong continued. 'And do you know where she had been? Where they had found her?'

No. Go on, please . . .

'On the bloody toilet,' Armstrong said. 'They found her passed out on the toilet. She had been on the nod. She was off her guts and had fallen asleep.'

Finally found, Brannigan didn't stumble out until 2.40 pm.

'All I had left was 20 minutes by the time they brought her out,' Armstrong said. 'And she was an utter mess. She didn't even come to me at first, even though I was her official visitor. She went to another table and kissed and cuddled three other people I didn't know. I later found out that she knew them from down Wollongong way, where she was from. She was there for about five minutes, like she was visiting them not me, until an officer got her and brought her over.'

Armstrong looked at her friend. She stared straight into her eyes. And she didn't like what she saw.

'Here eyes were pinned,' Armstrong said. 'She was slurring and completely out of it. In my opinion, she was on an opiate of some kind. It could have been anything, but I suspected heroin. I told her to pull up, go back to her cell. I told her to have dinner and go to sleep. I told her she was already wasted and didn't need any more, and to stop after that, because she was about to fuck everything up.'

Brannigan didn't listen. She didn't eat, she didn't sleep, and she was dead by 4 am.

KNOCK, KNOCK.

'Three days later a detective came to my home,' Armstrong said. 'I wasn't there, but a neighbour saw them and went to find out what was going on. Next thing I know I am getting a call at work.'

Kat . . . the police want to speak to you. They asked about your friend, Tracy. They said you're a person of interest and they need to talk to you. What have you done?

'I was like, "What the fuck is this about?"' Armstrong said. 'I was still grieving for the loss of my very dear friend, and now here I am being told by my neighbour that I was a POI [Person of Interest]. Seriously? I had spent the last three days crying myself to bed, thinking about what I could have done differently to save her. Was there anything I could have said that would have stop what happened that night? And now, well – the police are accusing me of *causing* it.'

Armstrong stormed out of her Sussex Street office in Sydney's CBD, and straight down the road to the police headquarters in Surry Hills.

A POI? Are you fucking serious?

They were.

'I went into the police station, and I had three police put it to me that I was the one who brought the drugs in,' Armstrong said. 'They told me they had statements saying I had.'

Statements?! From who?

'Lauren Ironside gave them a statement saying it was me,' Armstrong said.

'Look, she was in a desperate situation. She was two-out with Tracy and about to get bail that day. But she'd woken up and found her lover dead. She wanted to get out, was supposed to get out that morning, so she would have said anything to make it all go away.'

Said anything? Even that the friend who'd visited Tracy had given her the drugs? Yep.

'The police put it to her that I'd brought in the gear,' Armstrong said. 'And she agreed. She said Tracy got a visit from Kat, so it must have come from me. Tracy never would have told her where the drugs had come from. That's the first thing. She was a coy thing. She would have just said, "Who cares? Just take it." The second thing is that I would never have brought drugs in. I was trying to get her *off* drugs, because I was so worried about her. And, aside from that, she was under sanctions and being heavily watched. Why would I put myself at risk of going back in after all I had achieved and where I was heading?'

But there was a statement. She stood accused, a signature at the bottom of the police document.

'Lauren wrote that statement against me and the cops wanted a scapegoat,' Armstrong said. 'As far as they were concerned, I was an easy target because I was an ex-drug addict and a former inmate.'

But what about the video? Have you seen the video of my visit? Have you even bothered to fucking check?

'For once in my life I was glad that I was videotaped,' Armstrong said. 'They looked at it and could see no point where I could have given her the drugs. The thing that saved my arse was the video.'

Armstrong's grief then turned to rage.

Fuck you. Don't blame me. Do you want to know who's to blame? It's not me. It's those fucking pricks who'd locked Tracy in her cell knowing that she was off her face.

So she went to the media. And she said what she needed to say.

'Why wasn't Tracy put in an observation cell?' Armstrong said. 'That is the question. And it needed to be asked. She was off her face since the Friday and everyone knew it. I Dogged on my best friend to make sure they knew. But they did already. The police have statements to that effect. She was on sanctions, which meant they'd already suspected her of using drugs.'

Armstrong claims false testimony made by correction officers at the Coroner's Court inquest allowed the DSC [deputy state coroner] to escape blame for the drug overdose death.

'The officers made statements saying she was her normal self before they put her in her cell,' Armstrong said. 'They were blatant lies. The whole coroner's inquest was a sham.

They just didn't want a problem. The drug expert had never seen her, met her and made a judgment [that she was not affected by drugs] off a soundless video. I will never, ever forgive the jail and those officers for lying and not showing a duty of care to Tracy.

'Yeah ... She chose to [take the drugs], but they had a responsibility to make sure this didn't happen. I was the only one to tell the truth, and Lauren did too, eventually. The only ones to be honest were the crooks.'

But surely she made a difference? The DSC had been put on notice. Right?

'No,' Armstrong said. 'Three more women have died of overdoses in jail since. Nothing has changed.'

Overdoses a plenty, and drugs everywhere. But how do they get in? Ever heard about the 'hairy handbag'?

The Hairy Handbag

She slowly lifted the woman back onto the bed.

'You can't sleep like that honey,' she whispered, trying not to wake her friend. 'You'll get a bad back.'

She could have been as loud as she liked – the woman was wasted. She would have slept through a bomb blast.

Earlier that night, the now sleeping beauty had shown off her haul of drugs: a big bag of pills, successfully smuggled into the Emu Plains minimum-security women's jail.

How many did she take? thought the concerned house-mate, now tucking the girl in. *Too many* ... She reached down and pulled the crumpled bedding up to cover the zonked-out drug zombie. And then she screamed. The white sheets had turned red, soaked with fresh blood.

The house heavy, Linda, the hardest one of the four who lived in the domesticated prison house, rushed into the room. 'What the fuck! That's a shitload of blood.'

Quickly they shook the bloodied sleeper.

'Wake up!' screamed the heavy. 'Wake up. Now.'

Slowly, the drugged woman opened her eyes. 'What?' she muttered. 'What's wrong?'

Both her housemates were white with fear. They said nothing, instead pointing at the bloody mess of red on the bed, at what looked like a movie-set crime scene.

The girl sprang from the bed, the blood from her legs splattering the other two women and the floor. She stood and screamed, but not because of the pain . . .

'Who fucking stole my gear?' she cried. 'Which of you cunts took my drugs?'

Yep. That's right. This woman had stashed her drugs in her vagina before passing out. And now they were gone . . .

Victoria Schembri was the woman who had attempted to tuck the drugged-out girl back into bed after finding her body splayed and in danger of falling to the floor.

'I noticed the light was on and the door was open,' Schembri said. 'So I went in to check on her. I found her half-hanging off the bed, so I thought I would move her so she didn't wake up sore.'

That's when Schembri saw the blood.

'She had put her stash back up there before going to sleep,' Schembri said. 'Earlier, she had showed [the bag of drugs] around before putting it back in her "hairy handbag", which is prison slang for a vagina that you use to smuggle something in. Anyway, one of the other girls had gone in, put her hand up her and reefed out the stash while she was passed out. She was so wasted that she didn't even notice. The girl had literally shoved her fist up her and split her open. She had stolen the whole stash. I think it was smack, but I'm not sure.'

Linda, a renowned fighter, exploded. 'Which bitch did this?' she screamed, then stormed out and confronted the suspected culprit: the only other woman in the house.

'Linda cracked her,' said Schembri. 'She split her straight across the nose. Then she started yelling at her, asking what sort of low bitch would do something like that.'

The woman hit back. 'I didn't steal shit!' she shouted as she swung. And then the one with the bloodied legs and torn vagina joined in, attacking the alleged handbag thief too.

'It ended up in a full-on brawl,' Schembri recalled. 'I was terrified of violence, so I ran back to my room and locked the door. I had my back against the wall, shaking and pissing myself. I was terrified. My PTSD was so blown by this stage that I was just a mess. I used to wet myself all the time. Anytime there was a verbal, I would piss myself. I wore pads constantly.'

So, let's ask again – an inmate this time: how do the drugs get into prison?

*

The inmate chatted to her child.

'How you been, honey?' she asked, smiling. Today was the best day of the week: visits day.

Her son didn't reply.

'What's wrong, sweetie?' she asked. 'Don't you want to speak to me?'

Her pride-and-joy remained silent. Then he shook his head and pointed towards the next table, to an inmate visiting her man.

'What's he doing to her vagina?' he asked.

The inmate-turned-viper ferociously snapped her neck around.

Oh no. They aren't. No. My baby didn't just see that.

They were and he did.

'A guy was shoving a syringe up a girl's vagina in the visit,' the inmate said. 'It was blatant and it was horrible. But the girls have no shame when it comes to getting drugs in. They will do whatever they have to.'

The inmate turned her boy's head away from the horrifying drug transaction.

'I went and asked the officers if I could move to another table,' she said. 'You can't Dog on anyone, so I couldn't say why. I just said we had to move.'

Most drugs are smuggled into Australia's women's jails that way. Visitors are patted down and pass through an X-ray machine before entering the heavily monitored cafeteria-like area, but that doesn't stop drugs from getting through.

A husband, partner, friend or family member will bring the contraband into the visiting room and pass it to the inmate.

'It isn't very hard,' the prisoner continued. 'One way they do it is by having the girls put holes in the pockets of their pants. That lets their visitor reach straight into her pants so he can shove it straight up her vagina. That's the most common way. Women are constantly getting fingered during visits, so it just looks like they are getting into it. They literally reach around and shove it straight up their box.'

There is also the 'kiss and swallow', the 'sip and swallow' and the 'crunch and swallow', too.

'They would kiss their partners and swap a [drug-filled] balloon,' the inmate continued. 'Whoever brings it in keeps it under their tongue or in the back of their throat and gags it up before putting it into the girl's mouth with a kiss. They bring it in up their arse or vagina too, and go to the toilet and take it out. They will then put it in a bag of chips or a drink, and the woman swallows it.

'You get checked on the way back in, but you either keep it under your tongue or swallow it. You just shoot it back up later.'

The sister of one of Australia's most notorious criminals – a founding member of a murderous Sydney street gang – allegedly came up with an ingenious way to smuggle drugs into jail. Several inmates claim that she'd swap a drug-filled hair band with her prison-issue hair tie.

'She came up with the "scrunchy swap",' a former inmate revealed. 'Her visitors would come in with an identical scrunchy full of drugs, and they would simply swap them in the visits.'

There was also the thousands of metres of mostly guarded fence . . .

'At Dillwynia, there is a running track at the back that goes around the side,' the former inmate continued. 'It's just a cyclone fence, and that bit is mostly unwatched. That was the spot where they would throw drugs over the wall. [The inmates] would run past, shove it up their vaginas and off they'd go.'

Not all drugs were illegal, just illegally obtained.

'I had a really bad back, and the nurse wanted to put me on methadone,' said the inmate. 'One of the girls found out and told me that I had to go on it. That I had to let them give it to me. And then I had to hand it over to them. I was supposed to take it, throw it up and give it to them.'

Testing Times

Ever heard of a 'bodgie'? How about a 'tank'? Well, as a matter of fact, they are both the same thing: a disgusting but completely necessary prison item for anybody and everybody with a drug addiction. And it is one of the reasons why almost 85 per cent of women in Australian prisons, according to an estimate in one research paper, use drugs.

Drugs are illegal in prison, as they are in society, but they get into every Australian jail – and they are injected, smoked and swallowed. They are snorted, sucked and even taken by way of rectal suppository.

One way of combating what most officers describe as the biggest problem in jail is to test the inmates for drugs. Rather than stopping the drugs from getting in – *impossible, so they say* – is to find out who has been taking them and bust them retrospectively.

Genius. Great. Problem solved . . . Right?

Wrong.

'All we have is time on our hands,' said an inmate, who asked to remain anonymous. 'And we spend a lot of time thinking about how we can beat the system. Everything they come at us with, well, we find a solution to it. We can be a crafty lot when we need to be.'

So what's a 'bodgie'? What's a 'tank'?

Sure you want to know?

The cell door suddenly snapped open.

Shit. What's this all about?

Thankfully, at least for the junkie – the officer not so much – the infamous female inmate had stashed her fit about five minutes ago. The heroin was now safely swimming in her veins, the needle and gear tightly hidden in a covertly cut hole in her mattress.

Thank fuck!

'How ya doin', ya fuckin' junkie?' boomed the officer. 'Had your hit tonight? Look at ya! You're fuckin' flyin'!'

Floating on her mattress, the guard in the cell the only thing keeping her helium balloon-like head from bouncing off the roof and popping into the bliss of oblivion, the inmate attempted to focus on the threat now inching towards her bed.

'Nah,' she said, peering through pinhole pupils surrounded by bloodshot white. 'Not me, miss. I've been a good girl. Nothing for me. I'm clean. I don't take that shit anymore.'

'*Ha-ha-ha,*' the officer laughed. 'I am pissing myself. And that's exactly what I want you to do now. Come on, clean-skin. Let's go to the toilet and have a little wee-wee. Nothin' to worry about if you're tellin' me the truth.'

Shit. Is it in? Yep. Thank fuck.

The officer, now flanked by another beefy, not-so-chatty guard, handed her a glass container – the thing the inmates call a 'piss jar'.

'Her' ya go, sweetheart,' the officer said. 'Fill 'er up.'

The inmate fell onto the toilet while backing up – *smack-bang!* – her bum slapping against the closed seat.

Whoops. I'm fucking wasted.

She slowly, carefully stood before turning and placing the jar on the cistern. With both hands free, she fumbled around her waist, looking for the drawstring that held up her pants.

'Do you bitches want a show?' she slurred, pants and underwear now slack on the tiled floor. 'We can do a triple if you like? Go on. Come and have a lick.'

The officers did not move an inch.

'Shut up and piss,' one of them said. 'You know we have to watch.'

The inmate sat down and lowered the jar into the bowl. 'Nah, you're just a filthy bitch. You would love to suck on this snatch, wouldn't ya?'

The guard bit.

'Just fucking do it!' she yelled, staring the inmate straight in the face.

Yep. You beauty. Got ya!

She slipped her index finger from the jar as the guard yelled, leaving her pinky, ring and middle fingers holding onto the receptacle, now hovering an inch above the toilet water. She sent the free-roaming digit darting into her vagina. Her long fingernail did the rest.

Got it.

Urine rushed into the jar – a barrage at first, followed by a steady steam, and then a trickle. The inmate purposefully made sure she splashed the sides.

'Here ya go, bitch,' she said, handing the guard the piss-lashed jar. 'Drink up.' She pulled up her pants. 'Anything else? Blowie? A fist?'

The officer laughed again. 'See you when we get the results. You won't be such a smart-arse then.'

But the officer never came back ... The junkie's piss was clean.

How? She'd only just had a shot. She had just buried a needle into her arm, plunged the freshly smuggled heroin deep into one of her last remaining fully functioning veins. She had used the weekend before too, and the weekend before that. Well, she had used every weekend since that prick got drunk and didn't make it in for the Saturday visit.

But that was ages ago.

So, why did she come up clean?

'You know what a bodgie is right?' asked the woman at the centre of the story.

I shake my head.

'No?' she asked again, an astounded look on her now long-time sober face. 'A tank?'

I shook my head again.

'Ah, well,' she continued, 'that's how we beat the drug tests.'

She then went on to describe how a roll-on deodorant is transformed into a jailhouse drug-test beater that will have Lance Armstrong wishing he'd hired a couple of ex-Mulawa inmates instead of America's most expensive sport scientists.

'Yeah, we make them from the MUM bottles,' she said. 'That MUM deodorant. It has a pretty big lid that's the perfect shape for shoving up your vagina. So we all collect those lids and then get it filled up with clean urine.'

Clean urine? As opposed to that stinking yellow variety?
'*Drug-free* urine,' she explained. 'You get a woman who doesn't use drugs to piss in the MUM lid. There aren't many of those women around, but they have plenty of piss. And you can either stand over them [issue threats] or pay them to do it. Anyway, she pisses the clean urine into the lid of a MUM bottle and gives it back to you.'

Now, for some prison science . . .

'You get a dental dam [a sheet of latex that acts as a barrier between mouth and vagina during oral sex to decrease the risk of sexually transmitted diseases], which we get for free,' she said, 'or cling film, which we have in the kitchen, and you wrap it over the top of the lid. You then tie it off with a rubber band or some string.'

So, you now have a lid full of 'clean' piss?
'Yeah, the dam keeps the liquid in,' she said. 'Then all you have to do is turn it upside down and put it into your vagina. You put the side with the dam or wrap facing down.'

That's it?

'Basically,' she said. 'When they test you, a couple of screws will come up, hand you a jar and tell you to piss in it. They both watch, so you have to be a bit sneaky. You put the jar under your vagina, and with your fingernail you reach up and pierce the plastic. You use the hand that's already holding the jar so they don't get suspicious. The clean urine falls down into the urine jar and you hand it back to the officer. Easy.'

And that is a 'tank', a 'bodgie' if you prefer.

Easy.

'Yeah, the only hard part is making sure it's up your muff when you get tested,' she said. 'I would have a tank buried all the time. The only time I would take it out is when I slept. But even that was a risk. If they came in at night and found it, they would put you on sanctions. Getting busted with a tank was pretty much the same as getting busted with drugs.'

Drugs are rampant in prison. A Corrective Services NSW report, published in 2010, revealed the shocking truth. Here is a snapshot of the findings from the document, obtained for this book:

77% of females reported that at least one of their current criminal offences was related to their use of alcohol and/or other drugs. The overall rate was fairly uniform with that recorded in 2007–08.

Illicit drug use while in the community in the six months prior to the current prison episode was reported by close to three in four inmates (79% of females).

Use of 'heavy-end' drugs (i.e. heroin, amphetamine or cocaine) in the six months prior to current imprisonment was reported by more than one in two inmates (00% of females). Across the same time period, around one in three inmates (46% of females) reported that they had injected drugs.

Illicit drug use on at least one occasion in the current prison episode was reported by just over one in three inmates (39% of females).

44% of females reported experiencing drug withdrawal symptoms on reception for the current prison episode. The rate of reported drug withdrawal on reception showed a declining trend over the decade.

Prior participation in drug treatment was reported by 86% of inmates with a drug problem history (95% of females). This extrapolates to 74% of the entire sample reporting a history of drug treatment.

Just over one in three inmates (52% of females) participated in CSNSW psychology-based drug treatment programs during their current prison episode.

73% of females had received some form of drug treatment (either psychology-based or pharmacotherapy) during the current prison episode. One in two inmates (52% of females) reported receiving health promotion information during their current prison episode.

Around nine in ten inmates 89% of females had either been tested by urinalysis or searched by drug detector dogs during their current prison episode. Consistent with prior surveys in this series, from the range of contraband *detection strategies canvassed, urinalysis was rated as having the greatest drug deterrence effect.*

And you won't believe some of the things they do to score a hit in jail. Seriously. The next story is utterly disgusting.

You have been warned.

Purge

'Stick your fingers in your throat,' the veteran inmate said as she poked out her tongue before raising her middle and index fingers towards her mouth. 'Like this. It's easy.'

The woman who was being directed by the veteran inmate sat on the bed, hugging her knees. Received into Mulawa Correctional Centre just a week before, she rocked back and forth, staring blankly at her self-appointed prison coach.

'Yeah, nothing to it,' said another seasoned inmate, also in the newbie's cell. 'You just gotta stick it right in and you'll spew straightaway. But you have to stick them in pretty far. Past the back of your tongue. You kind of try to tickle the back of your throat.'

The first-time offender did not respond. She continued to rock back and forth, humming: *la-de-la-da-la.*

'Oi!' shouted the bigger of the two women. 'Are you listening to me?' The other woman moved in. 'She is fucking off her face. On another planet.'

She grabbed at the tiny girl, still rocking away and humming on the bed, and shook her. 'Wake the fuck up!'

The humming stopped, and so did the rocking, when the fresh fish was thrown to the floor.

'Well, looks like we'll just have to do it for you,' snapped the aggressor. The coach stopped coaching and attacked. She grabbed the back of the young girl's head, taking a fistful of hair. The girl did not fight back as she was pulled upright; she just looked at her attacker with empty eyes.

'Stick your fucking fingers in,' the aggressor demanded of her fellow attacker. 'Get it out of the bitch.' And with that she reefed open the jail rookie's mouth and jammed half a fist down her throat. She sent her fingers past the 'back of her tongue' and she 'tickled'.

Urggggh!

First the new inmate gagged.

Urggggh! Urggggh!

Her chest heaved and her head convulsed.

Urgggggggggggggggh!

And finally she vomited all over the cell floor.

The woman holding her hair tugged hard, sending the newbie crashing into the ground. 'Now that wasn't so fucking hard, was it?' she grunted, tufts of blonde hair between her fingers. 'But it would have been a lot easier if you'd done it yourself.'

The two attackers went to ground. They got on their hands and knees and crawled like wild dogs. And then they became animals, licking and sucking up the spew. They scrapped the stinking slush from the ground and shoved it into their mouths. They were rabid beasts, but no animal would eat spew for a hit . . . for a secondhand serving of methadone.

'They would force girls to go to the nurse and take methadone,' said a former Mulawa inmate who spoke under the condition of anonymity. 'And then they would make them spew it up so they could eat it.'

Yep. Seriously.

Another former inmate confirmed the disgusting practice of eating spew for a secondhand hit of the prison-prescribed substance used to treat withdrawing heroin addicts.

'I knew a girl who was forced to do it, she had never taken drugs in her life,' said the former inmate, 'but she was stood over and told to go to the clinic and get on methadone so they could make her spew and then eat it. That is the sick type of shit that went on. It was disgusting.'

So how does someone with no history of drug use convince a trained medical officer in prison to prescribe a highly addictive and destructive drug like methadone?

'Oh, that's easy,' she said. 'This girl just convinced the nurses that she needed it. She had never taken drugs in her life, but she told them she had been a heroin addict and wasn't copping. And, no joke . . . they gave it to her. They put her on the methadone.'

Model inmate Victoria Schembri alleges that she was offered methadone while incarcerated in Mulawa to treat a back complaint.

'They offered it to me, and I have never taken drugs in my life,' Schembri said. 'I had problems with my back and I was in a lot of pain. I told them about the car accident I was in when I was younger, and they suggested I go on methadone to treat the pain.

'I was like *what* – you want me to fuck my teeth, my liver and my bones, and become a drug addict because I'm in a bit of pain?'

Schembri claims drugs are over-prescribed in prison in a bid to keep the inmates subdued.

'They give methadone out like lollies because they want to keep everyone like zombies,' Schembri said. 'A medicated society is a subdued society. And it is certainly a medicated society in jail. Girls get on medication because they get harassed to go on medication. They do it for their own safety because they can buy themselves out of trouble.'

Schembri said another inmate asked her to get a prescription for methadone when she was first sent to prison.

'I was stood over by one of the toughest girls in the jail,' Schembri said. 'She was going to bash me if I didn't get medication. The only thing that saved me was [the outlaw motorcycle gang] the Rebels. She put the word out to see if I knew them, and I did. She would have bashed me for meds if I hadn't known someone outside. I would have had to go on meds if my ex-husband wasn't Rebel. Meds are a currency in prison. They can save your life. And they can cost you your life, too.'

Former inmate turned prison activist Kat Armstrong supported the claim that drugs are over-prescribed in prison. Armstrong said anti-psychotic drugs including Risperidone, Olanzapine and Lurasidone were prescribed to keep inmates docile.

'So many women are on them,' Armstrong said. 'Eighty-five per cent of women who are in prison are at some time prescribed anti-psych drugs. They make you sleep. They make you quiet. It's a control measure. All you have to do is ask for them and you get them. I have a relationship with a doctor who has worked in the prison system for 20 years, and she's horrified by what's happening. She actually came to us for help. That's pretty full-on that a doctor who's been working in the prison system for 20 years would have to come to a small advocacy agency like us for help.'

A government study into medication use in Australian jails confirmed that prisoners took prescription medications at a far higher rate than the general community. Conducted in 2015 by the Australian Institute of Health and Welfare, the study also found that a higher proportion of women prisoners than men took medication.

According to the report called 'Medication Use by Australia's Prisoners 2015: How is it different from the general community', 67 per cent of all female inmates in Australian jails were taking some form of medication.

The report also highlighted the use of anti-psychotic prescription drugs in prison.

'The types of medications where the difference between prisoners and the general community was the greatest were for those medications usually taken for mental health problems, addictions and chronic conditions,' the report said. 'These are areas in which prisoners are known to have poorer health than the general community. Compared with the general community, prisoners were nine times as likely to be taking anti-psychotics, more than twice as likely to be taking antidepressants or mood stabilisers, and four times as likely to be taking medications used in addictive disorders.

'Medications are an important element in the treatment of many physical and mental health conditions. Despite being relatively young, prisoners often have poorer health than the general adult community, and around half are prescribed medications of some kind.'

So does the report back Armstrong's claims? Well, yes and no. Prisoners have a higher need for medications, according to the study.

'The health problems experienced by this population are complex,' the report continued. 'Prisoners have higher levels of mental health issues, risky alcohol consumption, tobacco smoking, illicit drug use, chronic diseases, communicable diseases, disability and poorer self-assessed health than the general population. The health of prisoners is sufficiently poorer than in the general community, such that prisoners are considered to be geriatric at the age of 50–55. Prisoners also have a range of other issues that are related to their health, including poor literacy, intellectual disability, challenging behaviours and poor decision-making.'

The report also confirmed that both men and women were stood over for prescription drugs while in prison.

'Non-adherence to medications in prison, which may be either voluntary or coerced, is relatively common,' the report said. 'In prison, there is a concentration of people with substance misuse issues and reduced access to illicit drugs, so there is likely to be an increased misuse of prescribed medications, with prisoners seeking medication for hypnotic or euphoric reasons rather than therapeutic effects.

'In a small sample of people who had recently received opioid substitution treatment (OST) in prison, one-third reported being pressured to give their prescribed OST medication to someone else, and 44 per cent reported taking medications not prescribed for them while in prison. People misusing medications may manipulate and attempt to deceive clinicians in order to be prescribed certain medications, including visiting multiple clinicians. Close communication among clinicians can prevent this and may be easier to achieve in prison than in the community.

'In some instances, the medication-related considerations are highly practical and specific to a secure context. For example, some medications contain alcohol, which is prohibited in prison; capsules can be refilled and potentially reused; glass bottles can be used as weapons; liquid medications can be soaked into something and later traded; and some medications may interfere with prison drug-testing results.

'All these considerations can potentially impact on the availability of particular medications in the prison environment and how they are dispensed to prisoners.'

Sometimes the dispensing part can prove difficult. Well, at least when you get it wrong . . .

Purge, Part II

Roslyn reached out and snatched the plastic cup from the nurse's tray.

Mmm . . . Feels a little heavier today. Bonus.

With a quick flick of her wrist, the green liquid was gone as she shovelled the shot into her mouth and swallowed.

Yep. Definitely more today. Sweet.

'Thanks, boss,' said the inmate after devouring her daily dose of methadone, administered during the morning 'methadone parade'. 'You're the best.'

The nurse, who was walking towards the next cell, suddenly stopped. She almost dropped her tray filled with plastic cups of potions and pills.

Thanks? I'm the best?!

A siren sounded in her head.

Roslyn had never thanked her for anything. The best response – well, the only response – she had ever got from this drug-addicted prisoner was a belch after she swallowed the methadone and returned the empty cup.

And now she was saying 'thanks' . . .

Shit!

The nurse finished her rounds, delivering everything from painkillers to antibiotics, antipsychotics to vitamins . . . and, of course, methadone.

Maybe a little too much methadone.

She approached her supervising officer, her freshly emptied tray slightly unsteadied by her shaky hands.

'Hey, boss,' she murmured. He nodded as he shuffled through a pile of papers. 'Ummm . . . Hey, I think we should check on Roslyn's dosage of methadone. I have a feeling that it may not have been right.'

She suddenly had her superior's full and undivided attention.

'What?' he said, springing from his seat, papers returned to the pile of mess. 'Not right? Why, did she complain again? I've had enough of that woman. Did she abuse you again?'

The nurse put her tray down.

'Ummm, no,' the nurse said. 'That's the thing. She said "thank you" and then gave me a compliment.'

The supervisor's eyebrows rocketed towards the roof. 'Shit, that's not good.'

He marched out of the office and had hurtled halfway down the corridor by the time the door slammed shut.

'The officer went and reported it to the senior of the ward,' recalled a prison medical officer who was on duty at the time of the incident. 'The senior then went back to the Nursing Unit manager and made a series of enquiries. Anyway, it soon became evident that the wrong amount had been issued to the prisoner. She had been given more than she should have received.'

How much more?

'She'd been given a quantity that would see her overdose,' the officer continued. 'That was the opinion of the medical staff when the patient's records were reviewed and the exact amount administered had been established. We were advised that an overdose would occur considering the amount she had been given, and she would need to be hospitalised.'

Whoops! Hospital – that's not good. Heads are going to roll.

'We were told the only thing that could be done to assist her would be to induce vomiting,' the officer said. 'We had to bring [the methadone] back up.'

A posse of officers marched through the wing and confronted Roslyn in her cell. The inmate was sitting on her bed when they opened the door . . . giggling.

'I'm fuckin' off me head,' she laughed. 'I must've been a good girl, hey?'

The concern in the officers' faces could only be matched by the bliss on Roslyn's. She was grinning from ear to ear.

'Well, about that,' said the supervisor. 'A mistake was made this morning and you were given the incorrect dose of methadone.'

'Fucking oath I was,' she said. 'Thanks.'

The officer continued. 'Well, we now have a situation on our hands. We believe that the amount you have taken is going to result in an overdose, and we are going to have to take you to hospital.'

Roslyn giggled some more. 'Hospital?' she asked. 'Nah, I'm sweet. I'm flyin'.'

The officer shook his head. 'No, you are not. You're likely to have an overdose and your health is in serious risk. We're going to have to take you to hospital unless . . . '

Unless?

'Yes, unless you can make yourself vomit,' he said. 'We need you to have a spew for us.'

Roslyn started laughing. Hysterically. 'Yeah, right,' she said. 'I have the best high I've had in years and you want me to just give it up? To have a spew and make it all okay for you? Ha. Not happening, mate.'

The officer left the cell and reconvened in the office.

'What now?' asked the supervisor. 'How do we make her have a chuck?'

The nurse had an idea.

'Chocolate,' she said. 'She loves chocolate. Maybe she'll do it if we give her chocolate.'

They all smiled at the same time.

'So the senior officer ended up leaving the ward to go and see the deputy governor,' said the medical officer. 'He approached the deputy governor, told him the situation and suggested that it might be solved with a bribe. So, yeah ... He requested permission to bribe the FP [forensic patient] with a Mars bar from the vending machine in the visiting section.'

Stunningly, the 'bribe' was approved.

'Roslyn was escorted to a shared bathroom and encouraged to vomit six times and she would get the chocolate,' the officer continued. 'Roslyn obliged as three officers and four nurses looked on, smiling. Later, Roslyn was seen sitting on her bed, enjoying her favourite chocolate. And believe it or not the two officers involved received a department commendation for their quick actions!'

Yep. They were given an award for stuffing up and then solving the problem by making a bribe.

So why do they do it? Why do they eat spew? Smuggle syringes into jail in their vaginas? Dance with death every time they cop a hit?

Well, for that, we will need to speak to an addict.

4

THE (MIS)ADVENTURES OF AN ADDICT

Shit and Spew

'Ah, look at you,' the policeman said. 'You're a filthy bitch, aren't you? You're covered in shit.'

And he was all too right – Kat Armstrong was covered in brown, stinking, slushy liquid. The 19-year-old had shat everywhere: underwear, pants, legs, feet, all over the floor.

'That is fucking disgusting,' the officer said. 'You are just filthy.'

But Armstrong did not care. Not one bit. Not about the smell, not about the shit, and not about the prison she was now being drag towards.

She did not give a fuck about anything . . .

'I was too sick to care,' Armstrong said. 'I was withdrawing from heroin. The police drove me to Mulawa in the back of a paddy wagon, and I thought I was going to die. I had spew all over me. I had also wee-ed and pooed myself. I was covered in every type of filth you could imagine.'

Armstrong didn't care about the mess or the jail that loomed large in the distance, and the two police officers who escorted her to jail did not care about her.

Human waste? She was nothing more than a waste of a human, as far as they were concerned.

'The officers?' Armstrong said. 'Oh no. They would have let me die. They didn't stop once. They saw me, saw how sick I was, but they didn't give a shit.'

The police officers just wanted to get rid of her. They dragged her from the back of the paddy wagon and frog-marched her into the jail. They then handed her over as fast as the paperwork would allow.

Someone else's problem now. Shit. Hope I don't have to clean the back of the truck.

Armstrong fell to the prison floor.

'I was that sick,' Armstrong recalled. 'I could hardly walk when they got me out. I stumbled to the reception, and the [prison] officers looked at me and said, "Just another drug addict." They treated me like I was an animal.'

In fact, they treated her worse . . .

'Get your clothes off,' the officer barked. 'Strip. Get everything off now.'

Armstrong summoned all her strength and wrestled her shirt from her body. She then slowly, painfully, dragged down her putrefied pants. She looked at the officer, her eyes begging for mercy.

'What?' the officer screamed. 'Keep on going. I said strip. Take everything off. Get your underwear off now!'

Armstrong felt both sick and humiliated. She pulled off her underwear, soaked through with shit, and snapped off her bra.

The officer looked the smelly teenager up and down. Armstrong was a mere skeleton covered in flesh. Her breasts had been eaten away by the drugs she'd been living on. The widest part of her leg was her knee. Corrugated-iron ribs poked through her skin; stark white except for the deep, dark and plentiful bruises.

Sympathy? Of course not . . .

'Bend over,' the officer demanded. 'That's it. Squat. Now spread those cheeks and let's see what falls out.'

Armstrong complied.

'They put me in the shower after making me strip and bend over,' Armstrong said. 'I was so sick that I could hardly stand up. As sick as I was, I knew what was going on. It was the biggest shock of my life. I was thinking, *Are they allowed to do this? Is this normal?* I can't tell you how humiliating it was. To have them looking up your arse. I should have been in a hospital getting help. Not put through that.'

It had been two days since this five-year addict had jammed a needle in her arm.

'You get vomiting and diarrhoea when you're having withdrawals,' Armstrong said. 'And you just feel terrible.

It's like the worst case of the flu you've ever had but worse. You are totally lethargic. But you're not clouded like when you take ice and you're in psychosis. I was totally aware of everything that was happening.'

Initially oblivious to the prospect of being jailed in Mulawa, Armstrong was now scared. She would soon be terrified.

'I wasn't too concerned until I got there,' Armstrong said. 'The reception process shook me up. I didn't know anything about jail except for what I'd seen on the show *Prisoner*. I remember watching that show growing up and thinking it was bad, but it was nothing compared to reality.'

No, real-life jail was much worse. And now this teenager was wondering how she would survive.

'I was really scared,' Armstrong said. 'I was 19 and I weighed 47 kilos. I'm only five foot tall, so I was a skin-and-bone midget.'

Small, frail and scared, Armstrong did not even have the strength to complain when she was pushed into a shower.

'These two really tough female officers just chucked me in,' Armstrong said. 'They gave me a horrible little bottle and told me to put it in my hair.'

Armstrong opened the container and almost fell to the floor when her nostrils were assaulted by the smell of the suds. She looked down at the blue bottle with the pink label, trying not to breathe as she poured out its toxic contents into her palm, her knees buckling.

'What is this?' she found the strength to ask. 'It smells like weedkiller.'

The guard was not in a mood to converse. 'Put it in your hair,' she said. 'It's for lice.'

'It was horrible,' Armstrong recalled. 'It didn't matter that you didn't have lice, everyone had to put it in their hair. I remember it burnt. It stank and it felt like it was eating into your scalp.'

Arse-searched, industrial-grade bug killer administered, Armstrong was then handed a large plastic bag; in it was everything she would be allowed to own. The tough plastic ruffled as she stuck her freshly nuked hands inside, plucking out each item, one by one.

'There were two pairs of underwear,' Armstrong said. 'A bra, a sloppy joe, a pair of tracksuit pants and a pair of Dunlop Volleys. There were also two green t-shirts.'

Armstrong went straight for the underwear. No problem. Then she grabbed the bra.

'This isn't going to fit,' she said. 'It's like a size 16. Look at me. I don't even have tits.' The guard ignored her. 'And why are there stains on it? Yuk.'

The officer smiled. 'This isn't a five-star hotel. You don't get new things in here.'

Armstrong continued looking through the bag.

'Everything in there was used except for the undies,' she said. 'And nothing in the bag was my size. As I said, I was tiny and everything was too big.'

Some of it ridiculously so.

'I was a size eight in pants, and they gave me a size 14,' Armstrong continued. 'They were at least a foot too long. I had to roll them up so I wouldn't trip over. And the shoes – the cheap Dunlop Volleys – well, they were a size six and a half. I am only a size five, so they were flipping and flapping about. The only thing that fit me was the underpants. They were almost the right size.'

Armstrong thought the reception process was over. She was wrong. Soon she would have her clothes off again, this time for a nurse to search her skin.

'I was taken to what was called "the annex",' Armstrong said. 'It is now the hospital. I was put in a cage, and I waited there for about seven hours before I got to see the nurse. I had a medical assessment.'

The assessment went a bit like this:

Do you take drugs?

Yes.

What type?

Heroin, speed, cocaine if I can get it.

Are you having withdrawals?

Yes.

Well, unfortunately I can't give you anything. Are you on any prescription medications?

Yes.

Well, I can't give you any of them either. Here's a Panadol. Okay. That's it. Officer . . . the prisoner has been checked and is cleared to go to the wing.

Armstrong scooped up her bag from the floor and was led away from the poor excuse for a clinic and towards her new home. Towards the murderers, rapists and thieves, whom she would sleep next to with only a strung-up sheet separating her from them.

It was then that she decided she wanted to die.

'I wanted to kill myself,' Armstrong said.

The double doors swung inward and the terrified teenager, sickly and sore, was revealed to the wolves masquerading as women. They stopped stared, all 17 of them – some huge, some just big, some even small, but no one as diminutive as this five-foot-nothing skeleton fresh from the street.

And they liked what they saw.

Easy meat. She's mine.

Armstrong froze. *Oh shit.*

'This way,' the officer said. 'Come on. That's you over there.'

She pointed the first-time inmate towards a bed. Yep. Not a room, a bed. There were no bars, no doors, no walls. Nothing to keep the other 17 girls from attacking her while she was awake or, more likely, asleep.

'I was then taken to a place called Catchpole,' Armstrong said. 'It was a two-sided dormitory that was all open. You know, a bit like a hospital ward. There was an open bathroom and rows of beds.

'It was pretty scary going in because there was nothing stopping anyone from getting you. They could just come in and do something to you while you slept.'

Armstrong examined the room for threats.

Enemies from the outside?

No.

She didn't recognise any of the women. No one would want to get her for something she had done on the street.

Sexual predators?

Why would they want me? Look at me. I'm just another junkie.

Thieves?

Yeah. Probably all of them. But what have I got that they would want? Shit . . . smokes.

'I was given two packets of smokes with my clothes,' Armstrong said. 'Everyone back then was given a couple of packets for free, and after that you would have to get them in a buy-up. And I didn't know much, but I knew enough to know that everyone would be on me to get them as soon as the officers left and shut the doors.'

So what? Just give them the smokes.

'It isn't that simple,' Armstrong said. 'You could avoid a fight by handing them over, but by doing that you would be marked as weak. And they wouldn't stop there. Every time you got something you would have to hand it over. You would go straight to the bottom of the food chain.'

Armstrong steeled herself for a fight.

'I was getting ready for them to try it on me,' she said. 'And I decided there and then that I was going to fight. I was only little, but I knew how to box. One thing I'd learned how to do on the streets was fight. I'd been hanging out with some hardcore criminals, and I knew how to throw a punch. And I also knew you always had to fight back.

'If anyone was going to stand over me, even if I knew I was going to lose, I was going to have a go. The only way to stop them from standing over you was to stand up to them from the get-go. People will try it on, and people do try it on.

The only way I was going to avoid it was to fight back or ask to go into protection. And I was never going to be a Dog and ask to go into protection. That's not my go.'

So there she stood, all 47 kilos of drug-abused body, steeling for a fight. She slowly clenched her fists, pulling her fingers into her palms with all her might. Knuckles white, elbows tight, she walked towards her bed.

Any second now. Who will it be?

Movement to her left.

Shit.

A burly lady with shoulders that could have belonged to an NRL player was coming at her.

Armstrong got ready to swing.

'Shit,' came a voice – not to her left but her right. 'Kat? Is that you, Kat? Shit, girl. What you doin' here?'

The Rugby League look-alike stopped in her tracks. Then she turned and took off with the speed of a fullback.

Armstrong turned towards the familiar voice.

Thank fuck.

'It was a woman I knew from the streets,' Armstrong said. 'A woman I had done crime with outside.'

Not just 'a woman', but the toughest, meanest, most feared woman in the wing.

'She was an Aboriginal woman, and very well respected in the jail,' Armstrong said. 'And she came up and hugged me and said, "Ah, little Kat, so good to see you."'

Armstrong embraced the woman she had committed a robbery with a year or so before. And the other girls watched. And, more importantly, they took note.

'Everyone else saw it and knew not to touch me,' Armstrong said. 'We had done a whole lot of things together and had never been caught. All the others girls looked up to her, and right then and there I knew I was sweet.'

Her name was Kerry Anne Clarke. And Clarke was not a woman to be messed with.

'She was an older woman who had done a lot of time before,' Armstrong said. 'She was also very tough. She had shot at police and done armed robberies. All the other girls knew what she had done on the streets, and she was very high up in the chain.'

That one hug stopped Armstrong from having to fight for her smokes. Stopped her from having another woman jump in her bed at night and ask her for sex. It stopped her from having to fight for her life and bleed until she forged her own reputation. She was instantly respected.

'She took me under her wing,' Armstrong said. 'I was protected. If I she wasn't there then, I would have been stood over straightaway.'

Armstrong admits she was lucky.

'There are heaps of wings in that jail,' she said. 'And heaps of women. And I was placed in the one wing with a woman I knew.'

Not just knew. She was placed in the one wing with the one woman who was tough enough, and liked her enough, to make sure she did not have to fight 16 girls.

'Kerry was my saviour,' Armstrong said. 'The fact that she knew me from the outside and respected me told them that I was pretty tough in my own right. She wouldn't have had anything to do with someone who wasn't.'

*

Armstrong watched on, knowing the woman cowering in the corner could have been her. Three women towered over their victim, spit flying off their lips as they shouted, fists pumping the air.

'Nice shoes,' one of the women said. 'Nikes? How the fuck did you get them in here? You must be special, hey?'

The new inmate didn't say a word.

'Well, they're mine now,' the other woman said. 'Get them off and give them to me now.'

The young girl finally spoke. 'Give them to you? But that's all I have. I don't own anything else.'

The larger woman issued a warning. 'You want to get your head bashed in, little girl?' she said. 'Take them off now, or I'm going to smash you.'

Just admitted into the wing, all alone and in jail for the first time, the girl thought she could reason with the two toughies.

'But my mum gave them to me,' she said. 'They're special.'

Bang!

The first blow came without warning – a crisp, straight punch to the temple.

Bang! Bang! Bang!

Three more to the face. This time from one of the other two women, the second lady no less brutal. Her punches were clean and hard. The third woman stood back with her arms folded and laughed as the new inmate convulsed on the ground. The fourth blow had knocked out the fresh fish.

'But they kept on going,' said Armstrong. 'One jumped on her neck and the other one kicked the shit out of her while she was lying on the ground. It was sickening.'

Armstrong stood and stared, repulsed but reluctant to stand up to the standover women.

'She was just a young girl,' Armstrong said of the woman who was attacked by the gang of three. 'A first-time offender who had no clue what she was in for. A white woman and two Aboriginal women came up to her as soon as the dorm was locked and said, "Give me your smokes." She handed them over but then they went for her shoes.

'For some reason she had a pair of Nikes from the outside. She shouldn't have been allowed to have them. She should have had the prison Volleys, but she didn't, and that made her an even bigger target. She should have just handed them over.'

But she didn't. And she was bashed senseless.

'I thought she was going to die,' Armstrong said. 'One of the bitches was choking her while another was taking off her shoes. I wanted to jump in because it was so wrong, but I also knew that I should be minding my own business.'

Her protector, Kerry, gave Armstrong a crash course in Prison Survival 101. Rule 1.1: mind your own business.

'Kerry had told me to do my time – not everyone else's,' Armstrong continued.

'But, still, I wanted to help. I didn't know any of the women, but what they were doing was just wrong. They could have killed her over some smokes and a pair of shoes. But I'd been warned not to get involved in anyone else's politics, and I had to literally go against everything I believed in and just watch it happen.'

Armstrong doubts she could have stopped the attack.

'I would've been bashed as well if I'd gone in,' Armstrong said. 'The girl they were attacking couldn't fight at all, so it would've been me taking on three of them. I could have had a good go, but I don't think I would have had a chance unless some of the other girls in the wing joined in.'

They didn't. They just watched on, quietly talking about what they would have liked to do.

'Other women were saying it was wrong and wanted to do something too,' Armstrong said. 'But no one was willing to make that first move.'

At least not then, the first time it happened.

Armstrong stormed over to the three heavies who had been terrorising the same girl for four weeks.

'No more,' she said. 'You will leave her alone from now on.'

The biggest of the three shook her head. 'Yeah, fuck you. Who are you to tell us what to do? How are you going to stop us?'

Armstrong stood tall. 'Me and those seven ladies over there,' she said, pointing to a posse of veteran jailhouse brawlers, 'we're going to kick the shit out of you if you do it again. That's how we'll stop you.'

The three women laughed. But they never touched the young girl again.

'We stopped it eventually,' Armstrong said. 'We went up and told the girls that it was us against them. We told them that we're all here in the same boat and we need to learn to live together.'

The young woman had been stood over again and again after failing to fight for her Nikes.

'The week after the first attack, she got a full buy-up,' Armstrong said. 'She got back to the dorm and they were there to stand over her for it. It happened every week for four weeks. They took everything she had. After a month we decided it had to stop. That's when the group of us went up to them before the buy-up and said "When Natasha gets her buy-up this week, if you do what you've been doing for the last three weeks, then we're going to jump all over your fucking heads. It will be you three going to protection." They told us to fuck off, but they never touched her again.'

Armstrong said 'standovers' were a daily occurrence in jail.

'Women in a pack, when they are desperate ... well, they'll do some pretty fucked up things,' Armstrong said. 'And you can be stood over in other ways as well. Some women are stood over to do things like make cups of coffee and clean. You see a lot of the weak first-timers come in and become another girl's bitch. They'll be put in with a veteran of the system and they'll do the chores, clean the cell. That goes on all the time.'

Shelter? *Check*. Food? *Check*. Safety? *Check*. With Abraham Maslow's two lower orders in his famous 'hierarchy of needs' firmly secured, in no small part thanks to her jail-house enforcer friend Kerry, Armstrong was free to pursue the higher categories of 'human motivation'. And the highest order for Armstrong was, well, getting high.

She wanted drugs. And drugs she would get . . .

'I went looking for it straightaway,' Armstrong said. 'And I was told it was easy. There were drugs everywhere. I just had to wait until the weekend.'

Kerry, head held high and shoulders pinned proud, walked up to Armstrong. 'Hey, little Kat,' she said. 'Come with me. I've got something for you.'

Nudge, nudge. Wink, wink.

'Let's go to my room.'

Armstrong beamed.

'Four days after I arrived I got a hit,' Armstrong said. 'It was the weekend, and Kerry's best friend came in with a drop.'

Swoosh!

Kerry swiped the sheet shut, the rings sliding across the metal shower rod that formed the makeshift cell wall.

Kerry patted her bed. 'Sit here, love.'

Armstrong sat next to her friend. Two other women were in the room – one on the floor, the other joining them on the bed.

Kerry turned, plunged her hand into her mattress and pulled out a well-worn syringe. Drugs were easy to get in prison, syringes not so much. Soon a lighter was heating foil. The foil then turned frying pan, sizzling the score on top and turning it into boiling liquid muck. Kerry pulled back on the plunger and delivered the heroin into the syringe.

'You first, Kat,' she said. 'It's your welcoming gift.'

Armstrong jammed the needle in the first vein she found.

Fuck yeah.

Bliss. Oblivion.

Maybe prison isn't so bad?

It was all too easy, not to mention completely free. For once in her life, Armstrong didn't have to steal, beg or bash to score a hit.

'We were off our faces the whole weekend,' Armstrong said. 'There was plenty to go around. And that would happen every other weekend. Kerry's friend would come in with a drop and we would have a party.'

The officers did not patrol the wing once the door was shut. Not unless they had a reason to.

'We were locked in the dorm at night,' Armstrong said. 'They would shut the door at lockdown and not come back until muster. We could do anything we wanted once that door was shut. The officers wouldn't come in unless they suspected something. So we would just go into Kerry's "room", which we closed off with a sheet, and we injected.'

But there was only one needle. Not that Armstrong cared at the time. She happily plunged the metal tip into her arm, well and truly knowing that she was risking a death sentence.

'I shared that needle with four women the first time,' Armstrong said. 'And, yeah, it would have been used by others before. I didn't even think about sharing the needle. I had no problem with it.'

Drugs were easier to find than needles. Sad but true.

'There were no needle exchange programs back then [in 1988],' Armstrong said. 'And there weren't many needles around at all.'

Needles weren't so easy to smuggle in by way of your arse. Think about it . . .

'I was young and stupid, and I didn't think about where the needle had been or where it came from,' Armstrong said. 'I just wanted that fix.'

And Armstrong only wanted the fix, because after more than a week sober she didn't need it.

'I was almost clean by then because it had been six days since I had been in remand,' she said. 'I was over the withdrawals and I wasn't sick anymore. But I still wanted it.'

And so she had it.

'We used for two days until it was all gone. And I used the whole time I was there.'

And she kept on using when she was moved. She soon didn't need her enforcer friend to survive, or to find gear.

'I got classified and was sent to Conlon,' Armstrong continued. 'It was another part of Mulawa. I was put into a two-out cell with another woman who was a drug user. She was very similar to me. She had a similar upbringing and a similar story. And we were both drug addicts.'

Needless to say they 'got on'.

'Oh yeah,' she said. 'We got on it. It got harder to do the drugs in Conlon. Not harder to *get* the drugs, but harder to take them, because we were locked in cells instead of a dorm and there weren't many needles around. You could share them when you were in a dorm. But in the cells? Well, once you were locked in, then nothing was getting in or out.'

But Armstrong and her friends were crafty. Where there is a will (and an addiction) there is a way.

'We would quickly meet before lock-in and split up the drugs,' Armstrong said. 'So we would have gear but no needle, because at most times there was only one in the wing.

'So what we would do is send two people into a cell to have a shot just before we were locked in. Once they were sweet, we would then pass it to someone else and they would take it for the night. You would give the fit back the next morning.'

Feel sorry for the inmates? How about the people who guard them?

5

GUARDING THE GIRLS

Male in the Wing

The male officer was walking away from the kitchen when he heard the threat.

'You're dead, bitch!' a woman screamed. 'Come get a bit of this.'

Oh shit! Here we go again. I was hoping for a quiet day.

The officer pivoted on the spot and ran in the direction of the noise, towards the yelling woman, who was about to do who knows what.

'I knew it wasn't going to be good,' said the officer who worked at Mulawa Correctional Centre during the 1990s.

'These women could get up to some shit. Seriously, women are the absolute worst to deal with. I have worked in plenty of men's jails, some of the worst in New South Wales. And the thing with men is that they give you a level of respect. And mostly they can be reasoned with. But women? Oh shit. They are just wild. There's no talking them down or discussing things. You just have to jump straight in and wrestle them. And they're vicious things. They scratch, they bite, they hit. They don't care if you're a male. In fact, they probably go for you more because they know there isn't a lot we can do. A lot of them are men-haters anyway. There are heaps of lesbians in jail, and they don't need an excuse to try and rip into a fella.'

On this day in question, the officer was in Mulawa's Marshall Unit, and he was sure he was running headfirst into one of the scratching, biting, hitting types.

'Marshall is where they put the most violent girls,' he continued. 'All the fucking crazy ones. Mulawa was a big jail with about 300 prisoners all up. The prison was big. It had two sides – one known as Mulawa and the other Dawn de Loas. There was a plant nursery in the jail and a lot of the girls worked there, providing plants for Coles, Woolworths and Bunnings. You also had the sections that made headphones for the airlines. They repaired them.'

They also had a kitchen, the large inmate training room he was about to burst into.

Swoosh!

He stormed through the door without hesitation or fear. Well, without *showing* fear at least.

Oh shit! A fucking knife.

'Put it down!' he screamed. 'Drop it now.'

The woman looked away from the frightened girl she was about to stab. She deadpanned the officer.

'She looked completely mad,' he said. 'There was only hate in her eyes. She looked straight through me like I wasn't there.'

The woman snarled and turned back towards her prey.

Here we go . . .

The officer charged across the room towards the woman holding the twelve-inch carving knife. He quickly closed the gap and threw himself at the blade-wielding prisoner, the inmate ready and willing – a knife-thrust away from making a kill.

Smack!

He slammed into her with all his might. His weight and speed combined to create a formidable force. She went crashing to the ground, and so did the officer.

He looked down at the woman he was now on top of. She was still holding the knife.

Whack! Whack! Whack!

The officer launched three punches straight to the woman's head. The first of them – a heavy, bloody blow – probably knocked her out. But he had to make sure, so he landed two more, the quick double even harder than the first.

'You couldn't muck around with them,' he said. 'I just went in and pounded the shit out of her. I had to or she would have stabbed me. You have to forget everything you've learned on the outside. I was taught like everyone else never to raise a fist to a female. But these women, well, you can't think of them as females. They're killers. You won't last long if you hesitate around them or give them any concessions. Thankfully, that was the only time I had to bring down a woman with a knife. I had to go in and bring her down before she got the crim she was trying to stab.'

The officer said knife attacks were common in Mulawa during the 1990s.

'They had knives at that time,' he said. 'They had them in the kitchen area because some genius thought it was a good idea to teach them how to cook. They used to do their own cooking, and they had access to all sorts of knives – some of them as long as 12 inches. They would regularly stab each other in the kitchen. And sometimes they smuggled the knives out and did it in the wing.'

The officer saved a life when he took down the murderous chef. But he almost lost his job.

'They're not just hard to deal with because they're so aggressive and violent, but also because they're constantly making accusations against the males,' he said. 'Whenever you have to wrestle one of them, they will make a complaint. You have to prove your story against theirs whenever it happens. A female jail is an eye-opener for any male who goes in there. You have to be so careful. Each morning, when you did the six o'clock start, you would go in and do a head check, which means you had to unlock each door, just like you would in a men's jail, and you would check if they were still alive. Being a male, you would have to keep on calling out "male in the wing", so you wouldn't go in and catch them naked in the shower.

'They are always accusing us of perving on them or making sexual advances. But I can tell you it rarely happens. It's just a way for them to get some power against us and make us afraid to do our jobs. They are very cunning.'

A former inmate broke ranks to back up the officer who openly, albeit anonymously, admitted to punching a woman, before going on to accuse female prisoners of habitually making false claims against men.

'They often used force against women when I was at Mulawa,' she said. 'And to be fair, they had to for the most part. Sure, sometimes they went over the top, but this was a place full of particularly violent girls. A lot of the women were in there because they did cause trouble. It's where they kept Rebecca Butterfield and the worst, most dangerous inmates. All the classification fours [the highest risk category] were locked up in Mulawa.

'I saw plenty of situations where they had to jump on people. There were a lot of smart-arse girls who wanted to be tough. They would want to have a go at the guards, so the officers would have to get in and wrestle the girls.

'Usually it would be the women officers who would get into it. The males would sit back and only get into it as a last resort. It was difficult for the males because so many women would make complaints against them. Yeah, they were targeted a bit. The girls would go after them with false accusations.'

The former inmate recalled the most brutal incident she saw involving officers and an inmate.

'I saw officers throw punches on just one occasion,' she said. 'A girl was chucked to the ground. They had to do it because she was going nuts. She was off her head on ice, and it took four officers to hold her down.

'She was swinging an officer around on her back with this crazy drug strength before they were able to take her down.

They had to restrain her with cuffs – both on her wrists and ankles – and literally carry her away like she was a hog-tied animal. It took an officer on each of her limbs.'

Many suggest that male officers have no place working in women's jails.

Reverse sexism?

'I don't think they had any male officers until 1983,' said one male Mulawa guard. 'Some think there still shouldn't be. Lots of women, especially the crims, would like to have had just women staffing the jail. But the female officers know they can't always handle the women, and at times a male is needed.'

The same officer said female guards were essential in women's prisons.

'For sure,' he said. 'They seem to be able to handle them better in some instances. They can get on their level, I suppose, and some of the female officers I have worked with are better than most of the men.'

Another male officer, who has worked extensively in female prisons, said both female and male guards were needed to control Australia's worst women.

'The female guards are much more understanding,' he said. 'With male officers, it is all just yes and no. We just issue orders. With men that's fine. But women? Women want to talk. They want explanations and understanding. And you need to listen if you want to avoid a situation. It's never black and white with the women; it's always a conversation.

'I can't speak for every bloke, but for me it's hard work. They want to converse and I just want to do what needs to be done. I don't want to explain it or talk about it. But with women prisoners you can't say no and turn your back like you would with a man. Well, you *could*, but you risk having the back of your head scratched to bits.

'Force is used more on the females than the males. That is a statistical fact. It's all during strip searches. When they hide things it's called "boxing". They ram shit up their vaginas. They will put shit up there, the officers will see it, and the next thing you know they're wrestling. Every time we go in there is a use of force because the females are just so difficult to deal with.

'They always need to use force, basically because the inmates don't like being told what to do. I fucking hate dealing with women. I want to chuck a sickie every time I'm told I have a job in a woman's jail.

'Seriously. And I speak from experience. I have had plenty of them go off when I haven't thought I've done anything wrong. The women officers are so much better with that sort of thing. Is it a male–female thing? I don't want to say it is because I don't want to be sexist . . . but, yeah, it is. Women just do some things better than us.'

Another woman, a former inmate, shot down the whole 'women are better listeners' argument by heaping praise on the men who guarded her during her 11 years in hell.

'I met some amazing guards,' the now free woman said. 'And by far the two most amazing officers I ever came across were men. These two guys, who worked at Emu Plains, were friendly, polite and encouraging. They would even do things for us in their own time. They used to take us to a field outside the gates so we could exercise. They went out of their way to help you be a better person and to do things that would help you better yourself.'

The woman preferred being guarded by men.

'At most of the jails I would say there were more female guards then male,' she continued. 'And to be honest I found the male officers better. There were some seriously decent men working in those jails, especially at Emu Plains. They were very empathetic and would genuinely care about how you were and how they could help you cope. Some of them took particular interest in your family life, and others made sure you had the welfare you needed. One of them encouraged me to study and went out of his way to help.'

So were all the women officers butches and bitches? Baddies and bullies?

'Of course not,' she said. 'There were also some great women officers. One of the best was someone named Belinda, who ran the women and children's program at Emu Plains. She was every bit as good as any officer I ever met. I came across both men and women who were obsessively passionate about their jobs. About doing the right things.'

And they could be picked from a mile away.

'They were the ones who wanted to make sure you never came back,' she said. 'They wanted you to reform.'

And the others?

'Oh, the shit ones?' she asked. 'Yeah. There were the screws right at the other end of the chain.'

Females first.

'Some could be outright nasty, bitchy, pieces of shit,' she said. 'They made it their life's work to go and pick on people. And it was always the harmless girls they would pick on. They would buddy up with the bad girls – they absolutely loved the worst of them – and they would make life hell for little people. A lot of them were worse than the inmates. The bad officers didn't care about you and whether or not you came back. That's how I judged them. The ones I didn't rate would just look at girls when they got out and say, "I'll see you in a couple of months." They wanted you to fail.'

Victoria Schembri revealed that a vindictive female officer attempted to embarrass her and potentially place her in danger by revealing details of her often glamorous pre-prison live.

'Most of the officers were decent humans,' she said. 'Some of them weren't. One in particular was a complete bitch. This officer didn't like me. And she did her best to make life hard for me by bringing in a *Cleo* magazine that featured me and my husband. I'd done a feature with my man about healthy lifestyles or something just before I went in, and she found it and brought it into the prison. She put it on the coffee table in the officers' room, opened to the page with the story.

'She did it so they could put shit on me. She wanted to give everyone ammunition and told all the inmates about it. A male officer actually came to me privately and told me about it. He removed the magazine and apologised.'

The guards can become an inmate's worst nightmare. And the inmates? Well, one officer is still having nightmares about the day he found one dead.

'I saw it all,' said the male officer who had punched the woman with the carving knife. 'You name it. But the worst thing I reckon I had to deal with was a suicide. It might surprise you a bit but one of them really knocked me around and still gives me nightmares today.

'It was back in the mid-1990s. A female criminal had killed herself, and I was the one who found the body. She was in a unit and she'd hung herself on the back of the door. She had the noose around her neck, right on the door, so when I pulled the door open I bumped straight into her.'

Bumping into the dead woman was one thing. The blood was something else entirely . . .

'Before she hung herself she'd slashed her wrists and the back of her heels,' he said. 'There was blood everywhere. I slipped on the blood when I came in and grabbed onto the body to break my fall. I ended up pulling the body down on me. So there I was, covered in blood on a cell floor with a dead woman on top of me.'

Sleeping with the Enemy

The female inmate struggled with the box.

'Looks like the cows have been busy,' she said to the guard, who was hauling two boxes.

'Yep, the dairy farm is producing at capacity,' he said. 'I hope the girls like their Yogo. We better get it in the fridge before it goes off.'

The officer was sweating as he heaved the boxes, packed tightly with fresh yoghurt, towards the coolroom door.

He was relieved to be momentarily out of the sweltering sun, the coolroom about to provide a brief but welcome reprieve from the Western Sydney summer.

The officer had just started his shift at the minimum-security Emu Plains Correctional Centre, where there were more cows than bars and locking doors. Today he was helping a prisoner who had the prized job of transporting yoghurt, pasteurised and packaged by other inmates from the working dairy farm factory, to the fridge.

This job, more suited to a factory hand than a trained security specialist, was assigned exclusively to male officers; the boxes were heavy and the shelves were high.

The female inmate placed her box – bending her knees, not her back, as she had been shown – on the concrete floor beside the thickly insulated white sliding door.

'I'll get it,' she said, referring to the closed fridge door.

The heavy door whined as it ground over its metal runners. She slowly but surely pulled it open. The officer, still sweating as he held his two boxes, was hit in the face by a blast of refrigerated air. He paused for a second to savour the sudden cool change, the beading sweat on his brow now feeling like speckled frost.

Then he walked into the coolroom.

Bang!

Both his boxes went crashing to the concrete floor. Yoghurt exploded into the air, covering his feet, legs and the coolroom's walls in white gooey slop. The officer turned the same colour as the yoghurt.

'What's wrong?' said the inmate, who left her box on the ground and rushed into the coolroom. 'What happened? Are you okay?'

Oh shit!

She would have dropped her box too if she was still holding it.

They both stood in stunned silence, staring straight at the salaciously shocking scene. Two metres away from where they stood, hefty hips drove a hairy arse between long legs wrapped around his waist.

'What the fuck is going on in here?' the officer demanded.

The bum suddenly went still, the owner slowly turning to show his face.

'Oh,' said the officer. 'It's you . . . Shit. Why? *Shit.*'

Busted.

'Just get out of here,' said the exposed man, also an Emu Plains officer. 'I'll explain later. Shit. Don't tell anyone. You aren't going to tell? Please . . .'

He pulled out of the prisoner he was fucking on top of a stack of yoghurt boxes.

'Didn't you lock the door?' said the leggy inmate as she searched the floor for her underpants.

The offending officer was suspended without pay. His fellow officer hadn't dobbed – he hadn't had to.

'Everyone found out about it,' said a former Emu Plains inmate. 'It was big news. And I was really surprised by it because he was a lovely guy and I wouldn't have expected it from him.'

An investigation revealed that the officer had been having a sexual relationship with the inmate for several weeks.

'He had been giving her flowers, chocolates and gifts,' the former inmate said.

'That is how it started: giving her things and being nice to her.'

And soon they were having sex.

'They were fucking in the coolroom,' the former inmate continued. 'That's where all the yoghurts and dairy products were stored. They were busted in 2010, and it had been going on for a while. Another officer and an inmate busted them – walked in on them in the act. The girl who was having sex with him had a job [loading yoghurt], so they would've had plenty of time alone together to get away with it. Nobody would have known about it if they hadn't run past their shift.'

At least three officers – two male and one female – have been accused of having sexual affairs with inmates at Emu Plains since 2010.

'A lot of the girls are willing to have sex with a guard,' the former inmate continued. 'And lots of them do. The girl who got busted in the coolroom was a real quiet girl. She was shy, so it was bit of a surprise. But I think she was one of those people in jail who get real lonely and need some attention. I'm pretty sure she was in for a long time and that her partner had left her when she was sentenced.

'You don't understand how you miss human affection when you're in jail. Sometimes people just need that human touch, and I think that's why a lot of people who are heterosexual will enter into a homosexual relationship while in prison.

'You just get so desperate for that human touch, especially if you don't get any visitors.'

According to the inmate, some prisoners go looking for it.

'I never flirted to get things that I wanted,' she said. 'But lots did. A lot of the Asian girls in particular would turn it on to get attention and extra privileges. One of them would come out wearing her little singlet and tiny shorts and rub up against the glass whenever she wanted something. She would lean over and flirt, and some of the officers would eat it up.'

A male officer, who served at Mulawa during the 90s, said two guards were sacked for having sex with female inmates while he was working in the jail.

'Two male officers lost their jobs for it while I was there,' he said. 'And they were the ones who got caught – it does go on and a lot get away with it. Look, if you really want to do it you can. There are plenty of female inmates who will do it. There are plenty of girls who were pros or whatever, and they wouldn't think twice about having sex with an officer if they were getting something out of it. And there are others who are just horny. Some girls just want sex. I have had girls put it on me many times.

'One of the blokes I worked with got caught because he wrote the crim a letter saying that he hoped he hadn't got her pregnant. It was intercepted and he lost his job.'

So why would anyone risk a job for a root?

An officer who is currently serving spoke under the condition of anonymity, attempting to explain why officers were attracted to inmates.

'Is it the bad-boy image?' the officer said. 'Or the bad-girl image? I don't know. Some just have an attraction, and maybe they like to take risks. For others it's that sense of danger. I often wonder why they do it, why they have sex with prisoners. Me? I've never even considered it. But it goes on a lot.'

Former inmate Victoria Schembri said she was sexually harassed by a female officer at Mulawa Correctional Centre.

'There were quite a few lesbian officers who would try and put it on you,' Schembri said. 'Before I went in I thought it would be the male guards, but I had more problems with the female screws. One of the officers in particular flirted with us all. She would make inappropriate comments, and that was tough to deal with because of her position.

'You could handle other inmates, but it's difficult when it comes from a person with some power. You couldn't really complain about it. You would just have to brush it off and make it clear that you had a man and were only into men. I was always respectful, but at times I was very firm. But that's not to say all the lesbian guards were like that. One was absolutely lovely. She was a little body-builder chick, and she was just so friendly. Everyone knew about her sexuality, but she kept it behind a clear barrier and everyone knew where she stood.'

We've heard about the men who guard women and their sad stories, so it's only fair we talk to some women who have guarded men.

Girls Guarding Guys

The young officer walked through the wing; her eight-hour night shift had just begun.

'Miss, I really want to fuck you,' said a heavily tattooed man as she strode past an open cell.

The female officer stopped in her tracks.

'What?' she demanded, turning to find herself facing an infamous killer, now laughing as he skylarked with his equally murderous mates.

'Yeah? You want to fuck me?' she asked. The killer beamed as the attractive blonde guard stepped up to him. 'Well, I want to fuck you with a shotgun.'

The smile was slapped from his face, the shock proposition stinging more than any open palm to the cheek.

'*Ha, ha,*' laughed one the louts standing by the suddenly silent crook. 'She's going to fuck you up.'

Another one of his so-called mates joined in: 'Yeah. Bend over, man. She's going to give it to you with both barrels.'

The officer, only 20 and just months into her Corrective Services career, turned and walked off. She proudly wore the smile she'd stolen from the criminal, ripping it straight from his face with only wit and words.

'Oh, they can be bad,' said the officer, who began her career working in a maximum-security wing at an infamous jail, guarding some of the hardest, most dangerous, men on Earth. 'I've heard it all. They'll come right up to you and tell you the filthy things they want to do to you. They stand around with their mates and try to be the big guy. It's a bit like a bunch of pissed blokes at the pub on a Saturday afternoon when a good-looking woman walks in. One of them always wants to big-note by degrading her. The best way to deal with it is to put them down. You can put them back in their place pretty quickly with a few choice words.'

The officer, who asked to remain anonymous, is now a veteran corrections officer in a high-ranking position.

'I knew nothing about prisons when I joined,' she said. 'And I copped it from everyone. It wasn't an easy initiation.'

Think female prison officer for a moment. *What does she look like?* Got an image? *Yep.* Well, throw it in the bin. This lady looks nothing like the woman you just conjured up in your head. Forget television shows like *Wentworth.* The lady you have just met, and will soon get to know some more, is a knock-out. *Word association game again?* Think cosmetic clerk at a high-end department store.

Yep, now you got it.

'I got wolf whistles and propositions all the time,' the officer continued. 'We all did. That was part of the job. I can't tell you how many times someone told me they were going to fuck me. It was just the norm. They would tell you what they wanted to do to you, but at the end of the day you just have to brush it off. It's something you learn to ignore. You won't last long if you take it to heart. I guess having a thick skin is a necessity for the job. You get used to it. For me, the hardest part wasn't the crims – it was the male officers. They were arseholes. Pigs.'

Let's meet one, a hog who almost got her killed . . .

'I couldn't find him,' said the officer, referring to a male guard who had been rostered on to serve with her in the maximum-security wing. 'I was about half an hour into my shift and he was nowhere to be found. You would have two guards on each wing per shift back then, and I rocked up to work and was on my own.'

Where is the prick? There is shit to do. Should I start without him?

'I decided I had to find him,' she said. 'Not because I was scared to be in a wing with all these inmates alone, but because we had procedures and protocols to follow. I was more concerned about getting in trouble, or finding out that he had got in trouble. I was more concerned for him than me.'

So, all alone, one woman locked in a wing with 60 men – rapists, killers, thugs and thieves – she went from cell to cell and conducted her fearless search.

An inmate rushed towards her.

'Miss,' he said. 'What you doin' in here?'

She shrugged, completely confused by the comment. 'What do you mean? My job. Like always.'

The inmate was sweating, dishevelled and uncharacteristically concerned.

'Well, you have to get out of here,' he said. 'And you have to do it now.'

Again, she shrugged.

'Nah. Serious, miss,' he continued. 'They goin' to kill you . . . Run before it's too late.'

She enquired about her fellow guard.

'Did they get him?' she asked. 'Is he okay?'

The inmate's eyebrows came down, almost swallowing his big brown eyes.

'Ummm,' he stammered. 'He's gone already. He left before you even got here. He knew what was coming.'

The concern she felt for her colleague vanished – replaced in an instant with disgust and fear.

'I was going around looking for him and couldn't find him,' she said. 'He'd just disappeared. Word came to lock down, so I went up to do it by myself. Anyway, one bloke I was quite friendly with came up and told me to leave. He said get out now – they were going to take me.'

The inmates were getting ready to riot, and this attractive female guard was about to be taken hostage. And what do you think they would have done with her once they had dragged her into a cell?

'I was terrified,' she said. 'But I was equally pissed off with the officer I was supposed to be working with in the wing. He knew what was going to go down, knew what they were planning to do to me, and he left without telling me a thing.'

Trouble had been brewing for days. The inmates were warring between themselves, and what started as a fight was about to turn into a full-scale riot. The male officer had been worded up on what was about to happen, so he decided not to turn up to work.

'I found out later that there were big problems between the Asians and the Aboriginals,' she recalled. 'And it was all going to tee off that night. He got wind of it and did what he had to do, but he was only worried for himself. He was happy for me to be taken hostage, or worse. And I know he only did it because I was a woman. He couldn't stand the fact that there were women working in men's jails.'

Our lady officer had been working alongside this pig for a decade. She had proven she was every bit as capable as him. But he didn't care. In fact, he refused to even speak to her unless he had to. She got only grunts from him most of the time.

'He would swear at me sometimes or tell me off. That was about it. I'd been in the job for about ten years when this all went down, and he had barely said a word to me since I got there.

'The day I met him I put out my hand to shake and he refused. He just looked at me and said, "What are you doing here? You can't do this job. I don't want you here. Don't get in my way." He told me not to speak to him.'

The officer claimed that working with some male guards, one in particular, was worse than working with the criminals.

'The whole time I was there I would look at the roster, and if I was on a shift with him it was just horrible,' she said. 'It was so intimidating. He would talk to the crims before he would talk to me. He thought I was going to put him in danger because I was a woman and couldn't do the job.'

And yet he was happy to walk out on her, leaving her up against 60 criminals – ready to riot, rape . . . and maybe kill.

Dodgy Disguises and Daring Dates

The former officer pulled up the handbrake and killed the engine.

You'll be right. No need to be nervous.

She reached for the rear-view mirror and twisted it until she saw her reflection.

See? More Marilyn Monroe than Marie.

She adjusted her wig, making sure the thick blonde fringe was perfectly straight. She reached into the glove box and pulled out the pair of Ray-Bans she had just bought – dark lenses with a wide frame.

She faced the mirror again.

She didn't even recognise herself.

Genius. Easy.

She shut the door, calm and confident, before walking back into the jail for the first time since she'd been sacked.

Her heart raced as she approached the familiar face.

'Who are you visiting?' asked the man who she'd worked alongside for years.

'John Waldock,' she said. 'I'm booked in to see him at one o'clock.'

The burly man behind the desk raised both brows.

He knows. Shit. He knows.

But he said nothing, so she signed in using the fake name. She took a seat – heart pumping, palms sweating – and waited.

12.46 pm. She had 14 minutes before an officer would tell them it was time and put them through the X-ray machine. She knew the drill.

They won't let me in. They know.

But at 12.49 pm she was smiling at another guard – this one she didn't know – as she walked through the security scan.

My replacement?

The latch snapped open and she was soon through the first of the steel doors. She ignored the next group of officers; they ignored her.

Stop worrying. They don't suspect a thing.

She walked up to one of the four vending machines, her pulse now steady and her palms almost dry. She stuffed coins into the slot, not bothering to count, and mashed at the buttons. She pulled out the killer's favourite snacks – chocolate, chips and a Coke – and walked into the visits room. She dumped the junk-food haul on the small table and sat on a stool.

And again she waited.

One by one the inmates walked in. Rapists. Killers. Thieves. She knew them all. Not only their names and crimes, but what shampoo they liked, their favourite shows and football teams. She looked the third man who entered straight in the face. She had known this one for years. The criminal met her intense stare with blank eyes, his expression failing to change.

All good. You're sweet.

But where was *her* man?

She watched the clock as seconds turned into minutes. She began to sweat again as she studied the officers patrolling the room.

Are they looking at me? Or are they just doing what they're supposed to be doing?

She hoped they were searching for contraband. She hoped they were just watching sleeves for sneaky swaps.

Then he walked in. Her man. A callous killer named John Waldock.

The lifer, never to be released because of his sickening and senseless crimes, stood at the entrance to the visits room.

He looked left and then right. Then he looked straight ahead. Nothing. He scanned the room again.

'What are you standing there for?' an officer asked him. 'Who is visiting you?'

Shit. He doesn't recognise me.

'John,' she blurted, almost inaudible. She tentatively raised her hand, her digits hanging half-mast.

Nothing.

'John,' she said, louder this time, fully extending her hand.

'Her,' the criminal said and pointed. 'My girl.'

Waldock walked over and went straight for the chocolate.

The woman smiled. She had them fooled, or so she thought.

'We knew who she was,' recalled a former officer. 'A woman comes in wearing a wig for a visit with a bloke who never gets visits? Of course we knew. It was just sad. She had totally ruined her life for a killer who was never going to get out. We felt sorry for her more than anything else.'

Marie Sole was sacked by the Department of Corrective Services after it was discovered she had been sleeping with Waldock.

'I think she was pretty vulnerable,' said an officer who had worked with Sole at Bathurst Jail. 'She was one of the few female officers in the jail, and she was treated really badly by the male guards. All the females copped it, but Marie was treated particularly badly. And she didn't have much of a life away from the jail, either. She was a single mum who hadn't had a relationship with anyone for so long. No one gave her the time of day.'

But Waldock did.

'She suddenly found someone who was interested in her,' the officer continued. 'Waldock started chatting to her. He asked her how she was doing. He wanted to know her hobbies and what she was about. That's how it started.

'And he was quite a good-looking fellow. A clean-cut guy who used to work out. He was a lifer, and most of the lifers take care of themselves. They keep their cells tidy and are very organised. They need to be. It gives them a purpose, something to live for. They make the most of what they have. And I guess they also have nothing to lose by trying to get it on with an officer. They're never going to get out, so it's their only hope for having sex. And they have plenty of time to think about how to go about it. And with Marie . . . well, he obviously worked out what made her tick. He got inside her head.'

Sole threw her career away for the impossible love.

'She was such a hard prison officer,' the guard continued. 'Tough as nails and great at her job. She didn't have much else in her life, and she took her work very seriously. For her to chuck it all in for an inmate just didn't make sense. Not to us, anyway. The only one who could tell you why she did it is her. And from what I've heard, she's disappeared off the face of the Earth.

'All I can say is that it does happen. It happened to her, and it has happened to plenty of others. It comes down to personalities, and from what I have witnessed it is certainly the insecure ones who are the most vulnerable. Those who have no one on the outside get completely consumed by the job; the jail becomes their life. The people they deal with every day become the only people they come in contact with. And some end up taking it further than they should.'

Sole's career in Corrective Services, the one she loved so much, ended when she was caught in the act.

'They'd been watching her for a while,' the officer said. 'They had intel about what she was doing. It's hard to keep a secret in jail. The crims aren't known for being trustworthy people, and do you think this bloke wasn't bragging to his mates? It would be a pretty big badge of honour among them to be screwing a guard. Anyway, they had the intel and eventually sprung them having sex in the canteen.'

Stunningly, a fellow officer was revealed to be an accomplice.

'The officer she worked with allowed her to go up into the wing to see him,' the officer said. 'He covered for her. There are only two officers in a pod, and the cells are open most of the time. It was simply a matter of going on up to his cell. For an officer to cover for someone? I just can't understand it.

'It might never have happened without his help. Well . . . it probably would have. It's very easy for an officer to let themselves into a location where prisoners are. They can access cells whenever they want.

'You work very closely with these inmates – in activities, in the canteen, in industries – and you become very familiar with them. Still, it doesn't make any sense to me.'

Now, let's go meet the women who *really* need to be guarded.

The worst of the worst . . .

6

WORST WOMEN

Rebecca Butterfield
Fatal Attraction

Rebecca Butterfield, incarcerated in Emu Plains Correctional Centre, jumped from the sofa, dumping her knitting on the floor.

Finally. She's home.

Butterfield had spent all morning looping and stitching, a study of concentration as one row of wool turned into two, before becoming three, four and then more. But the knitting was a mere distraction, just a way to pass time.

I don't really need another scarf. And who else would wear a red one?

What she needed was now in the jail hut next door. The girl, *HER girl*, was finally home.

Butterfield stomped on her scarf-in-the-making as she charged to the kitchen. She no longer cared about her three hours of careful craft now that she heard the voices coming from next door.

She pulled a knife from the wooden block – *schwing!* Not just any average knife, but the biggest, sharpest one she could find. The one she used last night to slice through a thick, tough rib eye. She looked down at the sparkling blade. And then she smiled, ear to ear . . .

Butterfield burst through the door and stormed past two fellow inmates, knife in her hand, hate in her heart. They said nothing. They did nothing. Bluce Lim-Ward was standing in the lounge room. She had just returned from working the morning shift. Lim-Ward didn't even see Butterfield coming. Her back was turned, completely oblivious to the beast with the blade closing in fast.

Whack!

The first blow sliced straight through skin and rib, and then cracked bone.

Whack! Whack! Whack!

Back meat, spine and then rib again.

Whack! Whack! Whack! Whack! Whack!

The blows rained down – short, sharp and powerful. In-out, in-out, in-out, the blade turned machine gun.

Whack! Whack! Whack! Whack! Whack! Whack! Whack! Whack! Whack! Whack!

Butterfield was relentless in her stabbing and slicing, saying nothing as she buried the blade into flesh, reefed it out and did it again. Blood spurted from the wounds, spattering the carpets and walls, pooling on the floor. Butterfield was drenched in blood too. But that didn't prevent the maniac from unleashing another 15 blows. Lim-Ward was dead well before Butterfield stopped. Then the crazed woman continued to cut up the corpse.

Butterfield stabbed Bluce Lim-Ward 33 times, all up, just months before the business woman from the Philippines was set to be released for her fraud-related finance crimes. In broad daylight, at a minimum-security facility, in front of at least four witnesses, the ticking time bomb murdered in cold blood. When the gruesome deed was done, she went back to her room, picked up her yarn, her needles and finished knitting her scarf.

Ivan Milat, the notorious 'Backpacker Killer', is not the most feared person in prison. Nor is it Martin Bryant – the man who went on a killing spree in Port Arthur, claiming 35 lives in what was the worst ever mass shooting in the world at the time. No, the one who needs chains, leather straps and a full-time posse of guards is not even a man. The most dangerous inmate in Australia is Rebecca Butterfield – a self-mutilating murderer infamous for slicing guards, inmates and herself. And for the very first time, we can reveal the full details of the jailhouse slaughter that saw her become the first inmate to be kept locked up indefinitely under a controversial new law. Meet Australia's worst inmate, the first woman to ever have her file marked 'too dangerous to be released'.

Jill pretended she didn't know who the new fish was.

'Hi,' she said, outstretched hand ready to shake. 'What's your name? I'm Jill.'

The 28-year-old newcomer, already a veteran of the NSW corrections system, smiled. There was nothing sinister about the grin, nor her sparkling blue eyes, but her face was scarred – fleshy zippers sliced deep into her skin.

'Rebecca,' the other woman said as she shook her hand. 'Rebecca Butterfield.'

Jill nodded. She already knew. Word went out about this self-harmer long before she arrived to the Emu Plains. Exclusively for low-risk female offenders after male inmates were moved out in 1994, the sprawling farm was home to a fully functional working dairy.

'I met her in 2002,' said Jill. 'It was right at the back end of my sentence. I'd heard about her before she came out. I don't think she'd been in the system for that long, but she certainly had a reputation. We all knew that this Rebecca girl was coming out. She was known to be crazy.

'I was told that she'd assaulted two officers during a stint in Mulawa and been sent to Long Bay Hospital to be treated for a year a two. The superintendent approved her to come to Emu Plains, despite her record and reputation. I was on stage two at the time.'

Jill was ordered to mentor the newcomer. *What the fuck? It's taken me ten years to get this job.* Jill, who had been locked up in several jails across the state, held a supervisor's position at the dairy farm. Each morning she would rise at 4 am, exit through the unlocked door of her accommodation 'hut' and present herself for her shift.

'They brought her over to me and told me to show her how to do my job,' Jill said. 'I had one of the best, well-paid jobs in the prison, and it had taken me a long time to get it. I used to look after the calves. I was about to get out and someone else was going to be getting the job, but I couldn't work out why they were giving it to this upstart who had bashed guards.'

No one doubted the stories. *Fuck . . . Just look at her face.* She had to be bat-shit crazy, *surely.*

'She struck me as weird straight-up,' Jill said. 'You could see she was a nut case just by looking at her – she had scars all over her face – but I tried not to judge. I decided I would be alright to her if she was alright to me.'

So Jill gave the girl a chance. She had to. *What other choice did she have?* The boss of the jail had assigned her Ms Zipperface, and who was she to argue? Surely the boss knew about her history and wouldn't put her or fellow low-risk inmates in harm's way. *Right?*

'I'm from Moree,' Butterfield said. 'Way out bush. Where are you from, lady?'

Jill smiled. 'I'm a country girl, too.'

Jill began reconsidering her original assessment of the latest woman to join her on the farm.

'Maybe we had enough in common for this to work,' she said. 'She could hold an intelligent conversation, and we seemed to have a bit in common. I mean, we were all surprised that she had come straight out of Long Bay and was put in a stage two area, but she seemed pretty normal.

'Still, I was never going to turn my back on her. There had to be something wrong with her, given that she'd assaulted officers and set herself on fire.'

Yep, they all knew about the time this Butterfield set herself alight. That she smuggled in a match and torched her cell, and herself.

Jill hoped there was more fiction to the stories than fact. Unfortunately, each and every tale about Butterfield was true.

Rebecca Butterfield looked across the yard, eyes firmly focused, finger raised.

'Who's that?' she asked.

'Her?' Jill shrugged. 'That's Lou.'

Butterfield said nothing. Instead, she simply sat and silently stared.

The woman who had caught her eye was Bluce Lim-Ward. Bluce was considered a model inmate and had not so much as had an argument since being sent to the softest slammer in Sydney.

'She's cute,' Butterfield said, finally breaking her silence. The big girl licked her lips.

'It was a fatal attraction,' Jill said. 'A *real-life* fatal attraction.'

Yep, a deadly infatuation involving mimicry, menace and finally murder.

'Lou was a sweetheart,' said Jill. 'She was only in there for something very minor, and she was getting ready to go home when Rebecca came into the jail. It was really fucking strange what happened. There was no reason for it at all. Rebecca took to her straightaway. She started asking all these questions about her first before actually finding the courage to go and talk to her.'

Lim-Ward was immediately kind to Butterfield. She suspected nothing. And why would she? Lou was a wallflower. A pretty little thing who liked to cook and water the garden.

'I don't know what Rebecca's intentions were to this day. I don't know why she formed this thing for Lou. Maybe she wanted to have a relationship with her? Something sexual? She could have been that type. But it was definitely a fatal attraction. Shit got really weird, really quick.'

It started with singlets, shorts and hairstyles.

'She began doing her hair the same as Lou,' Jill said. 'If Lou wore it up, then Rebecca did also. It wasn't much at first, but we noticed. She started parting her hair to the same side as Lou, cut it to the same length.'

And then came the clothes.

'We don't have too many dress options in jail. But if Lou came out wearing a white singlet and Rebecca had on green, Rebecca would rush in and get changed into a white one too.'

Lim-Ward was oblivious to the threat this woman posed. She embraced Rebecca, thinking that she had a kind, new friend. *An admirer?*

'Lou didn't have a bad bone in her body,' Jill said. 'She'd worked as the assistant of industries. She wasn't a drug user or a fighter. She wasn't anyone who demanded attention. She was a real good cook and liked to work. I remember having a big talk to her about her future, and she was going to go back to the Philippines to spend time with her family and start her life over.'

But she would never get the chance.

Rebecca waited . . . her knitting keeping her busy until it was time to kill.

'I'll never forget that day,' Jill said. 'She spent the morning knitting. She liked to knit. She did that until all the girls from industries came home from work. We lived in these little houses. We were in stage two, so we could come and go as we pleased. Rebecca was in the non-smoking house, but she would always go next door to the smoking house. I think it was called House 11. It was very communal and friendly – not what you'd think a jail would be like.'

Well, at least until Butterfield brandished the knife.

'She walked in with a huge meat knife in her hand,' Jill said. 'Not a steak knife but a much bigger one – like a small meat cleaver. We were all stage two, as I said, and we were allowed to have a knife set in our house. Rebecca had pulled the biggest one out.'

And now she was steaming towards Lou. She ignored the other girls as she charged in, an unstoppable train carrying a full freight of pain.

'And then she stabbed Lou,' Jill said. 'Right in the back. I heard Lou scream. It was horrible. It's sending shivers down my spine recalling it now. Oh, how I wish I could forget it.'

Jill, frozen with fear, watched Butterfield tear through Lim-Ward's skin, into back, bone and bum.

'There was blood flying everywhere,' Jill continued. 'Rebecca just kept on stabbing her in the back. I don't know how many times she stabbed her. I saw her stab her three or four times before I could even manage to scream.'

Jill, a tiny woman and recovering heroin addict, knew she could not overpower the marauding behemoth. So she ran.

'I went straight out of the hut and up to the office to get help,' Jill said. 'Another girl ran with me. We screamed as we ran: *help, help, help!*'

The pair got to the main gate and frantically bashed into the intercom, pressing, pounding and praying for help.

'But no one answered,' Jill said. 'There were no officers in there. There was a big superintendent meeting on that day, and they were all over meeting the mothers with their babies. It took about 40 minutes for an officer to answer the knock-up [prison slang for raising an alarm].'

Bluce Lim-Ward was dead when paramedics arrived, having suffered 33 stab wounds.

Butterfield tried to escape through the laundry when security finally turned up.

'A disturbing feature of the case is that there was absolutely nothing to suggest the victim did anything to provoke the prisoner,' said the judge who convicted Butterfield of the murder. 'Her past history indicates that unprovoked and violent attacks upon others have been part of her criminal history.'

'We were heartbroken,' Jill said. 'We built a little memorial garden for Lou out the back. It was all because Rebecca was jealous of her. Well, that's what I think. They left the bloodied house untouched for eight weeks. Guys from the South Coast, blokes in periodic detention, ended up being sent up to clean it.'

Butterfield was taken back to Long Bay Correctional Complex, where she spent her days strapped to a bed, thick-gauge leather straps holding down our very own Hannibal Lecter.

'She's a disgusting thing,' Jill said. 'I have no doubt she's the most dangerous woman in the system. She would be the most dangerous *person* in the system. She can never get out. She's a cold-blooded killer and a complete nut.'

Butterfield is not a popular woman. Crazy, sick and psychotic are the words most commonly used to describe the killer.

And another woman witnessed the crime.

'I was there from December 2002 to 2003,' said the former Emu Plains inmate. 'I knew both Rebecca and Lucy, and I was there on the day of the murder. I'll never forget it.

I was supposed to be working outside on that day, but I chucked a sickie. I wasn't feeling well, so I stayed at home. I lived not far away from hut number ten, and I heard it and saw it. It was just horrific. I can't tell you how much I regret chucking that sickie. They locked the place down. All the people who worked outside the compound weren't allowed back in. I should have been one of the girls outside, not one of the ones looking at Lucy's cut-up body.'

And while not defending Butterfield, by any means, the inmate gave a reason to explain why she may have been so unhinged on the day of the grisly murder.

'It was a horrible crime and there's no doubt she's a complete nut job. But one thing I will say in her defence is that they hadn't given Rebecca her medicine the day before she killed Lucy. I spoke to her the day before, and she told me that she went up to the medical hut three times and told them she needed her medication, but for some reason the screws wouldn't give it to her. So I know for a fact that she wasn't properly medicated on the day she killed Lucy. That's not an excuse, but I reckon it played a part.'

The inmate said the department was never held to account for its role in the death.

'No questions were ever asked about the medication, from what I know,' the inmate continued. 'Surely there should have been an investigation. And Rebecca shouldn't have even been there in the first place. She had a history and it was recipe for disaster. Put a nutter in a place like that and then don't give her the nutter drugs she needs? It's a disgrace.'

The department did take measures to ensure there would not be a repeat of the murder that turned hut number ten into slaughterhouse.

'A lot of things happened after that,' the inmate continued. 'I mean, the knives for one thing. We had real knives until that incident. After that they were taken away. We were given plastic. Security was tightened as well.'

Creating History

The NSW Supreme Court agreed with Jill's assessment of Butterfield in 2016 when it made the historic – and unprecedented – ruling to keep the murderer locked up beyond the completion of her maximum sentence. Dubbed the 'most dangerous inmate in New South Wales', Butterfield was deemed 'too dangerous to be released'.

The NSW government successfully applied through the Supreme Court to keep Butterfield behind bars for at least another five years under the *Crimes (High Risk Offenders) Act 2006* on the grounds that she is an 'unacceptable risk' of reoffending.

'The combination of disorders and psychoses suffered by the defendant and her history of criminal violence leads inexorably to the view that if unsupervised this defendant would more likely than not commit a serious violence offence,' Justice Stephen Rothman wrote in his findings.

'There is evidence that some of the defendant's threats of self-harm or engagement in self-harm are premeditated for the purpose of forcing officers to enter her cell and enabling her opportunities of violence against the officers.'

Yep, like the time she cut her self to smithereens with a smashed-up light globe . . .

The highly trained escort guards, these ones based at Goulburn's Supermax – Australia's most secure jail – travelled to Sydney with a mission to take a woman to court.

A woman?

Usually it was the serial killer Ivan Milat going to one of his never-ending appeals. Sometimes it was the feared Brothers 4 Life gang leader Bassam Hamzy. But today it was a low-profile murderer called Rebecca.

Wearing bulletproof vests and equipped with just about every non-lethal weapon known to man, the guards walked into Long Bay Jail and slowly moved towards their assignment.

'It's very, very rare for us to have to take a woman on a high-security escort,' said one of the officers. 'In fact, Butterfield is the only woman I've ever had to escort, and the only one I've ever *heard* about having an escort. And this woman . . . well, she's worse than any man I've ever had to move.'

Bang! Bang! Bang!

'Time to go, Butterfield,' said one of the escorts as he pounded on the door.

The inmate was completely compliant. 'Sure,' she said, almost sweetly. 'What took you guys so long?'

The guards slowly, carefully and calmly searched the cuffed woman. She had chains on both her feet and wrists.

Take every precaution with this one.

'Clear,' shouted one of the specially trained officers. 'All clear.'

They marched her through the heavily fortified door.

'See, Rebecca could be a charmer when she wanted to,' said the officer. 'That was part of what made her so fucked up. She would try to lure you in, and you could sometimes forget what a nut she was. Anyway, we took her down to a holding cell at the other end of the jail while we made our final preparations.'

Bang! Bang! Bang!

The guard pounded again, same knock but different door.

'Yep, okay,' said Butterfield. 'Just give me a minute, please.'

Shit!

'You know something is wrong when she asks for more time,' said the officer. 'That's a warning that she's about to do something.'

Boom! Crack!

The officer saw the exploded fluorescent light tube on the concrete floor of the cell as he rushed through the door. He was already too late. Butterfield jumped down from the chair she had used to remove the plastic cover from the light, before taking out the metre-long, high-wattage tube.

She was now clutching the still-intact end of the tube, waving the improvised weapon around like a Jedi would a lightsaber. She pointed the jagged, razor-sharp end at the intruding officer.

'Stay back or I'll shove this straight into your face,' she snarled. 'I mean it.'

And she was serious. Butterfield had a long history of violence, attacking guards with boiling water, cups of piss, blades and even fire. Now it was skin-shredding glass.

'She just looked at us and said, "You are not taking me to court," in a terrifying voice,' the guard recalled. 'She threatened us before turning on herself.'

Butterfield stared down the officers as she slowly pushed the jagged end of the light tube into her skin. She pressed hard on the soft flesh next to her elbow, spraying blood against the wall and she drove it deep.

'She proceeded to cut herself from the crook of her elbow all the way down to her wrist,' the officer said. 'It ripped her forearm to pieces. There was blood and flesh everywhere.'

The guards jumped on the gore-covered woman after she dropped the improvised weapon, her body quickly going weak from blood loss.

She looked at the guards before she fainted and said, 'See, I told you I wasn't going to court.'

The officers took her to the hospital instead.

Butterfield is among a rare group of prisoners who are known as 'self-harmers'. They will turn even the most harmless objects into a weapon and stab, cut or bash themselves to death if they get the chance.

Here is a short history of Butterfield's attempts to self-harm, taken from her official prison file obtained for this book:

2003 – Ms Butterfield requires stiches after cutting her own throat.
2004 – Ms Butterfield requires more stiches, again cutting her own throat.

2005 – Ms Butterfield tries to hang herself, then cuts her own throat.

2006 – Ms Butterfield cuts her throat and almost bleeds out.

2008 – Ms Butterfield severely bangs her head and inserts item under her scalp.

2009 – Ms Butterfield headbutts a wall 105 times and splits her skull open.

'The headbutting episode was just brutal,' said former PO Grant Turner, a man who spent much of his time guarding and escorting the troublesome inmate. 'She just started bashing her head against the wall.'

Soft at first – *tap . . . tap* – then faster and harder – *bang, bang, bang.*

'She opened herself up,' Turner said. 'She smashed through her skull and left blood and bone all over the wall. One hundred and five times was the official count, but it was probably more. I don't know how she didn't suffer brain damage. I'm sure I saw some grey matter on the floor.'

Another former Long Bay Jail officer recalled the head-busting attack: 'I saw her afterwards. It was fucking horrible. Her skull was ripped right open, and you could see all the way through to her brain.'

So, why does she do it? Why would a woman, officially deemed to be sane – *yes, sane* – open up her own skull against a wall?

'She does it for attention,' the guard said. 'After her head was stitched up, she ripped open the stiches and jammed things into the wound. For whatever reason, she doesn't feel pain, and she'll hurt herself any way she can for a thrill. She once tried to cut off her own head with a toilet seat. She sat with her head in the bowl, slamming the hard seat into her head, as if it were a guillotine. You would not believe some of the things she has done.'

Turner said Butterfield was the worst inmate he encountered during his long and distinguished career. 'She constantly had wounds. She would hurt herself so we'd have to take her to the hospital, and more often than not she would attack us when we arrived. She also attacked nurses, doctors – anybody who she could get near.

'Everybody in the system knows Rebecca Butterfield. She's absolutely off her chops. You could never go one-out with her. Apart from the attacks, she would also make accusations against you. In the end, she could not have access to anyone or anything. She's just too dangerous.'

Another guard agreed with Turner's damning assessment.

'She doesn't really care about her reputation,' the current serving officer said. 'She's just nuts – and really, really dangerous. Part of the danger is because she's so manipulative. You can be lured into trusting her, and as soon as you let your guard down she attacks. A flick just switches somewhere in her head, and all of a sudden she's trying to slit your throat.

'I hope they never let her out. She will kill as soon as she can get her hands on somebody. She just gets off on it.'

Butterfield was originally sentenced to serve just six years for stabbing a neighbour in a row over a man. She could have been out in just three years had she not embarked on the most extensive and vicious attacking spree that the Australian jail system has ever seen.

The internal prison report obtained for this book makes for shocking reading. These are some of the convictions mentioned in the document that was given to the Supreme Court during the successful 2016 bid to keep her locked away for at least another five years.

The offender was convicted of Common Assault and sentenced to a period of six months imprisonment. The police facts state that the offender assaulted a Registered Nurse whilst she was receiving treatment for a self-harm wound at Bathurst District Hospital.

22 August 2000: The offender was convicted of Common Assault and Assault Occasioning Actual Bodily Harm (AOABH) and sentenced to a fine of $500 and four months' imprisonment. In relation to the Common Assault, the inmate physically assaulted a correctional officer and the AOABH offence involved the inmate using a jagged piece of plastic to cut a correctional officer on his face as he opened her cell door.

11 February 2008: The offender was convicted of Assault Officer in Execution of Duty, Assault Occasioning Actual Bodily Harm (x2) and Common Assault and was sentenced to four periods of fixed imprisonment not exceeding six months. The details were as follows:

- *Common Assault – Ms Butterfield kicked a nurse whilst she was receiving treatment at Westmead Hospital.*

- *Assault Officer in Execution of Duty – Ms Butterfield threw a cup of urine at a correctional officer.*
- *Assault Occasioning Actual Bodily Harm (x2) – on one occasion, the inmate threw a cup of boiling water at a correctional officer and the other charge involved the inmate assaulting a correctional officer during a strip search.*

2006: It is further noted that in 2006, Ms Butterfield was charged with Assault Officer in Execution of Duty and Assault Law Enforcement Officer (not police) Inflict Actual Bodily Harm, which involved the offender assaulting a correctional officer, however this charge was discharged under Section 32 of the Mental Health Act.

Butterfield was designated an 'extreme high-security' prisoner by the Corrective Services Commissioner in 2003 after she made threats against guards. 'Extreme caution should be exercised when dealing with this inmate,' said the report. 'Butterfield has made a threat to kill an officer. In particular, she has directed this threat towards female officers.'

Another entry reads, 'Exercise caution on all external escorts. Butterfield is able to remove handcuffs.'

But she assaulted so many people despite the warnings, including kicking a pregnant nurse in the abdomen while receiving treatment. Some very serious questions need to be asked about why Butterfield – the inmate who now lives in complete isolation – was sent to Emu Plains minimum-security prison in 2003.

The entrance to the minimum-security Emu Plains Correctional Centre at the foot of the Blue Mountains might be leafy, but it's far from a holiday destination. (STEPHEN COOPER/NEWSPIX)

Welcome to Dillwynia Correctional Centre in South Windsor, NSW – a sterile environment, but infamously rough. (SARAH RHODES/NEWSPIX)

Dillwynia comprises one of three correctional facilities at the John Morony Correctional Complex in Western Sydney. Bushfires rage outside the gates, symbolic of the inferno within. (TOBY ZERNA/NEWSPIX)

A 1993 aerial view of the Mulawa Correctional Centre for women (now known as Silverwater Women's Correctional Centre) in Silverwater, NSW.
(ROY HAVERKAMP/NEWSPIX)

The forbidding courtyard of the behaviour management single-person cells at Dillwynia Prison. (SARAH RHODES/NEWSPIX)

The lounge room at Dillwynia Correctional Centre, the first purpose-built women's prison in NSW. (SARAH RHODES/NEWSPIX)

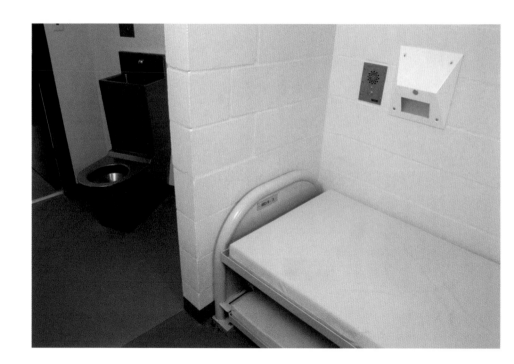

Inside a single-person cell at Dillwynia. The idea of bathroom privacy is something you leave at the gates when you enter.

Necessity is the mother of invention. Various items used to smuggle in contraband, from a corrections press conference at Silverwater Jail. According to one retired corrections officer, 'The easiest way to get it in was to just go and throw a tennis ball containing a bag of drugs over the fence.' (JEFF HERBERT/NEWSPIX)

Rebecca Butterfield was labelled the state's most violent inmate and controversially had her sentence extended by five years because she represented an 'unacceptable risk' of reoffending. The worst of her crimes committed while inside Emu Plains was the murder of fellow inmate Bluce Lim-Ward by stabbing her 34 times.

The old abattoir at Aberdeen, NSW, where cannibal killer Katherine Knight once worked. She'd apply those knife skills in the skinning and decapitation of her partner John Price in October 2001. (BOB BARKER/NEWSPIX)

The house in Aberdeen where the gruesome tableau of John Price's mutilated body was discovered: seated on the lounge, legs crossed, drink in hand. (STEVE TICKNER/NEWSPIX)

The kitchen where Knight cooked Price's head and parts of his body, and later plated them with roasted vegetables. (BOB BARKER/NEWSPIX)

Screen grab of police escorting Knight, convicted of the horrific crime and the first woman sentenced to life imprisonment without parole, from Muswellbrook Courthouse, NSW, in 2000. (FAIRFAX PHOTOS)

Lucy Dudko leaving the Downing Centre Court, Sydney, after being handed the guilty verdict for hijacking a helicopter and breaking her boyfriend, Robert Killick, out of Silverwater Metropolitan Remand Centre in 1999. (RENEE NOWYTARGER/NEWSPIX)

Police officers speak to pilot Tim Joyce, who was hijacked at gunpoint by Dudko and forced to land his helicopter in the prison's exercise grounds. (TRACEE LEA/NEWSPIX)

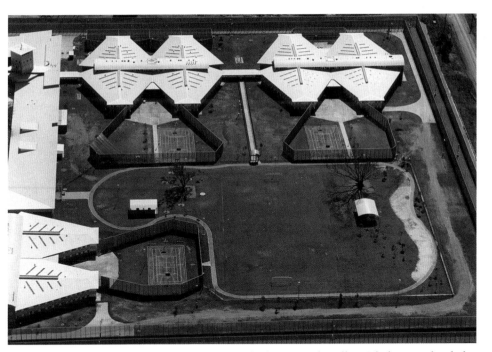

Aerial view of Silverwater and the exercise oval where Joyce's Bell 47G helicopter landed after it was hijacked. (TROY BENDEICH/NEWSPIX)

Lucy Dudko leaves Dillwynia Women's Correctional Centre in Berkshire Park, Sydney, after serving seven years for the jailbreak. She now leads a quiet life, no longer in contact with Killick. (CHRIS HYDE/NEWSPIX)

A woman scorned. Kathy Yeo was sentenced to 24 years in prison for shooting her ex-lover Christopher Dorrian before cutting off his head. She was reported to have smiled as the sentence was read.
(BILL COUNSELL/NEWSPIX)

Yeo's former boyfriend, Raymond Galea, received eight years for accessory after the fact, having helped to dispose of Dorrian's body. Only the severed head was ever found, when it washed up in a sports bag along Cooks River in Sydney's south.
(CRAIG GREENHILL/NEWSPIX)

All in the family. Belinda Van Krevel, sister of Mark Valera, outside the courthouse in August 2000. Valera was found guilty of the 1998 mutilation deaths of Dapto storekeeper David O'Hearn and former state MP and Wollongong Mayor Frank Arkell.
(CRAIG GREENHILL/NEWSPIX)

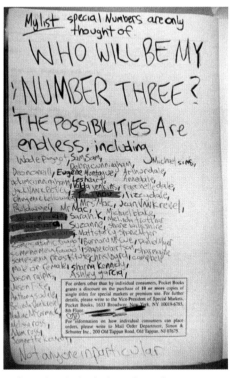

Convicted double-murderer Mark Valera leaves NSW Supreme Court in September 2000. Of the more gruesome details to emerge from the crime was the use of O'Hearn's severed hand to scrawl satanic symbols on the living room wall.
(CHRIS HYDE/NEWSPIX)

Valera clearly had plans for at least a third victim, as evidenced by the names he recorded in a book. Disturbingly, the line at the bottom reads, 'Not anyone in particular.' (CRAIG GREENHILL/NEWSPIX)

Police talk in front of the house where the body of Belinda and Mark's father, Jack Van Krevel, was found hacked to death with a knife, a tomahawk and fire poker. During the horrific crime, Belinda lay in silence with her two-year-old daughter in the next room.
(JIM ALCORN/NEWSPIX)

Belinda Van Krevel outside Parramatta Court in Sydney in 2010. She served six years for convincing her former partner Keith Schreiber to kill her father, whom she believed to be molesting a family member.
(STEPHEN COOPER/NEWSPIX)

Maddison Hall leaves Dillwynia Women's Correctional Centre on 22 April 2010, after being released on parole. Hall, as Noel Crompton, was jailed for the shooting murder of hitchhiker Lyn Saunders in 1987 before undergoing a sex change while in prison. (CAMERON RICHARDSON/ NEWSPIX)

Maddison Hall updates her Facebook profile after her release, embracing life on the outside.

Victoria Schembri, the 'Model Inmate', enjoyed life as a movie extra, sometime stripper and men's magazine starlet before she was convicted and sentenced to serve a maximum of seven years in jail in 2009 for claiming more than $500,000 worth of bogus GST refunds. She is pictured here in 2014. (ANDREW DONATO)

Schembri exchanged the string bikini for the prison-issued greens. The mother of three's nightmare began from the moment she entered the jam-packed Surry Hills police station holding cell. (COURTESY VICTORIA SCHEMBRI)

Top: 'In the holding cells beneath Downing Centre at Surry Hills, my life flashed before my eyes. My daughters' faces, my son's face, just kept spinning as the tears that streamed down my face blurred my ability to see, let alone think straight. How was I, a mother, ever going to survive in a cell, surrounded by murderers, rapists, drug dealers, fraudsters and violent criminals?' (PHOTOS COURTESY VICTORIA SCHEMBRI)

Centre, Bottom: Schembri eventually found herself drawn to many of her fellow inmates, wanting to learn their stories and share her own. It was this lack of judgement that found her becoming close friends with Katherine Knight, who is known affectionately in Silverwater as 'Grandma'.

Kat Armstrong, a founder of the Women in Prison Advocacy Network (WIPAN) with ex-prisoner Lynda Kelleher (in pink). Armstrong, a former Mulawa inmate, pulled herself out of a life of crime to serve as a prisoners' rights advocate and a mentor for women who want to turn their lives around.

'She should have never been there,' said Jill. 'Everyone, even all of us, knew who she was and what she was capable of. I can never understand why she was put in with us stage twos. Lou would be alive today if they would have kept her locked up in Long Bay where she belonged.'

Katherine Knight
Don't You Know Who I Am?

Australia's most infamous female killer did not get the reaction she was expecting. *Maybe even hoping for?*

'Did you hear what I said?' she asked firmly, her face full of surprise. 'I said my name is Katherine Knight.'

Victoria Schembri's expression did not change. 'Umm, okay,' she said, her hand still extended, waiting for the woman to return the greeting. 'Yeah. I got it. It's nice to meet you.'

Knight raised her eyebrows, shrugged her shoulders. '*Mmm,*' she murmured. 'That name doesn't ring a bell?'

What's this chick on? Does she think she's famous? Is she famous?

'No, I don't think I've heard of you,' she said. 'Sorry.'

Shit. Should I know her? Am I pissing her off? Is she an actor? Maybe a singer? Definitely not a model . . .

'Seriously, you've never heard of me?' Knight asked again.

'Katherine Knight?' Schembri shrugged and shook her head.

'Geez,' Knight drawled. 'Have you been living under a rock?'

Knight finally extended her hand, and they shook.

'I like you,' Knight said. 'I think we're going to be friends.'

And she was right. Australia's most infamous female inmate and the first-time offender, in for fraud, became friends. Best friends.

'I was very close to Katherine Knight,' Schembri said. 'We had an extremely special relationship, one of the closest I've had in my life. I know that sounds strange, but it is what it is.

'She came up to me when I first got to Mulawa and introduced herself. She was in complete shock when I didn't react to her name. She thought I was having her on. But, honestly, I had no idea who she was. She was obviously used to a reaction, but she didn't get one from me.'

Knight let go of Schembri's hand following the short, soft shake.

'Seriously?' Knight took a step back, her eyebrows still raised. 'You don't know me. Don't you watch TV? Have you read a newspaper in the last five years?'

Schembri, comfortable despite her identity ignorance, shook her head again. 'No, sorry. I'm not too interested in the rest of the world. I have had a lot to deal with lately. I really don't know who you are.'

Knight beamed. 'Good,' she said. 'According to the papers, I'm the worst woman to have walked the Earth. I'm a monster. I'm the only woman never to be released.'

Schembri considered her next move. *What do they say in prison movies? Are you supposed to ask what they did? Or not? Shit, I forget.*

Oh well, bombs away . . .

'Umm,' Schembri mumbled, her eyes looking at the floor. 'Well, so what did you do? What are you in for?'

Let's find out . . .

The Knight of the Long Knives

Knight pulled the tray from the oven.

Not bad. About 30 minutes to go.

The vegetables, carefully seasoned and oiled, had softened in the 180-degree heat. She placed the sizzling tray back on the shelf and shut the oven door.

Time for the meat . . .

Knight delicately sprinkled the freshly butchered cuts of meat, first with salt and then pepper. The finely sliced slivers were white and tender, and she drizzled them with a thin layer of olive oil.

Knight placed the meat on a pre-warmed, lightly greased roasting tray, one-by-one peeling the fresh cuts from the heavily scarred wooden chopping block and arranging them on the surface of the tray.

Soon the meat was in the oven, slowly roasting.

Twenty minutes?

Knight wasn't sure. She had never cooked human before.

The slivers of meat, expertly taken from her own lover's bum cheeks with a paring knife, looked like a serving of chicken breast from the grocery story.

How long does chicken take? Twenty-five minutes? Yeah, that's about right.

The meat and vegetables were sorted, or would be when the oven timer went *ding*, but Katherine Knight was far from done.

This was to be a banquet.

The 45-year-old mother of four grabbed her favourite stirring spoon and sunk it into the simmering stew. She dug through the vegetables and stock before prodding at the prize: John Charles Thomas Price's head. The face flesh had softened, some floating alongside the cut-up potatoes and pumpkin.

Satisfied with how the feast was coming along, she walked into the lounge room to look at where her dead partner, or at least the parts of him that weren't roasting, boiling or hanging from the meat hook attached to the living room door, sat.

She had placed the headless – and skinless – carcass on the father-of-three's favourite single-seat recliner.

She looked at the butchered corpse. She wasn't satisfied.

Mmm. Not quite right.

She crossed his lifeless legs and placed a drink bottle in his stone-cold, stiffening hand.

Perfect.

Soon it was time to set the table – just two places. They were reserved for Price's two children. Along with the usual knives and forks, salt and pepper, she placed two notes on the table, one for each of the children. What did she write? Well, we will never know. The details of the handwritten letters were suppressed in court.

The contents of another note were, however, revealed. Knight placed a third letter on top of a picture of Price.

'Time got you back for rapping [raping] my douter [daughter],' she wrote. 'You to Beck [Price's daughter] for Ross for Little John [Price's son]. Now play with little John's dick John Price.'

Knight plated up. Braised human buttocks placed next to baked potato, pumpkin, beetroot, zucchini, cabbage and yellow squash. All topped with gravy. She made three plates, but the third never made the table. She hurled the head and vegetables into the backyard after eating a portion of the meat.

Cooking complete, table set, Knight then swallowed a fistful of pills – fluvoxamine and promethazine – the drugs sending her to sleep.

Knight stabbed John Price 37 times after waking up the miner for sex. At 11 pm on 29 February 2000, dressed in black lingerie she'd bought that day, she delivered the fatal blow by plunging a blade into his chest. She then used her extensive collection of knives, and abattoir-trained meat-cutting expertise, to butcher, cook and serve his body.

'The prisoner, who had for many years worked as a meat slicer in abattoirs, skinned Mr Price's body,' Justice Barry O'Keefe summarised during Knight's trial.

'This was carried out with considerable expertise and an obviously steady hand so that his skin, including that of the head, face, nose, ears, neck, torso, genital organs and legs, was removed so as to form one pelt. So expertly was it done that, after the post-mortem examination, the skin was able to be re-sown onto Mr Price's body in a way which indicated a clear and appropriate, albeit grisly, methodology. One small segment was left in place – the skin on the left upper chest.

'At some time after Mr Price had been skinned, the prisoner hung his pelt on a meat hook on the architrave of the door of the lounge room, where it remained until it was later removed by investigating police.

'As is apparent from the fact that his head and neck were removed as part of one entire skin, Mr Price's head was in place at the time he was skinned. However, at some time between the time when the body was moved into the lounge room and skinned and about a time before 7.30 am on 1 March 2000, the prisoner decapitated Mr Price's body and at some stage arranged it with the left arm draped over an empty soft drink bottle, and the legs crossed.'

Knight removed Price's head with surgical precision, and with a knife she had sharpened moments before slicing into his neck and severing his spine. A sharpening block was found next to an assortment of her favourite knives.

'The evidence of the Medical Examiner establishes that the decapitation was effected at the C3/C4 junction and was done with a very sharp knife,' Justice O'Keefe said.

'The removal was clean and left an incised type wound. To remove Mr Price's head in such a way required skill, which was consistent with the skills acquired by the prisoner in the course of her work as a meat slicer. It also required a steady hand at the relevant time.'

And the human steaks?

'Not only was Mr Price's head removed but parts of his buttocks were also sliced off,' O'Keefe said. 'The excised parts of Mr Price were then taken by the prisoner to the kitchen and at some stage, after she had peeled and prepared various vegetables, she cooked Mr Price's head in a large pot together with a number of the vegetables she had prepared so as to produce a sickening stew. The contents of the pot were still warm, estimated to be at between 40 and 50 degrees Centigrade, when examined by police during the mid-morning of 1 March 2000. This supports the conclusion that the cooking of Mr Price's head took place at a time into the early morning of 1 March 2000.

'The pieces which had been cut from Mr Price's buttocks were baked in the oven of the premises by the prisoner together with the other vegetables she had peeled. The gruesome steaks were then arranged on plates together with the vegetables which she had baked and left as meals for the son and daughter of the deceased, accompanied by vindictive notes to each in the handwriting of the prisoner.

'A third piece was thrown on the back lawn, whether for consumption by dogs or for some other purpose is not revealed in the evidence.'

Cutting, cooking and consuming a corpse – that is what Knight did to Price on the night of 29 February 2000.

But why?

On the day he was murdered, Price took out a restraining order against Knight. On his way to work – just another day in the mine – the 46-year-old made a pit-stop to Scone Magistrate's Court. He told the court that he had fears for both the safety of himself and his children after telling Knight she could no longer live at his house.

Price then went to work and told his colleagues of his concerns: 'If I'm not here tomorrow, it's because she's killed me.'

Price finished his shift and went home. His two children weren't there. He made a phone call and learned that Knight had sent them to a friend's house for a sleepover.

Oh, well. They're fine.

Price spent the evening at a neighbour's house before going home. He went to bed at about 11 pm. Knight arrived sometime after 11 pm. She let herself in and watched TV before waking him for sex. Despite the Apprehended Violence Order (AVO) and the murder prediction he made to his colleagues, Price obliged. He willingly had sex with Knight, rolled over and went back to sleep. Police found his corpse eight hours later.

Detective Sergeant Bob Wells arrived at the scene shortly after police broke in to find Price's head in a pot, his skin hanging from a meat hook and the rest of him in a chair. Police had gone to Price's house at 8 am after he failed to turn up to work.

'It's an image I'm still trying to come to grips with today,' Wells said.

An army of officers were called to the house of horrors to work out when, who, how and why?

'His death was as a result of multiple injuries to various organs of his body, secondary to multiple stab wounds,' said NSW Supreme Court Judge O'Keefe. 'The post-mortem examination revealed that Mr Price had been stabbed at least 37 times in various parts of both the front and back of his body. There may have been more wounds inflicted, but the extent of those found and the subsequent acts of the prisoner in relation to Mr Price's body rendered it impossible to know how many more there may have been and in particular the number of wounds which may have been inflicted in the area of his neck.

'Many of the wounds were deep and extended into vital organs. These included the aorta, both lungs, the liver, the stomach, the descending colon, the pancreas, and the left kidney, the lower pole of which had virtually been sliced off.

'Blood was found splattered and smeared throughout various parts of the house and in a pool, which was quite deep, and measured one metre by two metres. This pool was in the hallway of Mr Price's home. At the time the police arrived on the morning of 1 March 2000, the blood in it was not fully congealed and had dried only at the edges.

'The blows which inflicted the injuries to Mr Price were in a pattern that spread from the upper part of his body to his buttocks and below and had been struck with some considerable force by a knife which had a long blade. A butcher's knife, which answered such a description, was found adjacent to Mr Price's body. In addition, a butcher's steel for sharpening knives was found on a lounge chair next to his body. A sharpening stone was also found. It was open on a bench in the kitchen, quite close to the sink and stove. It had clearly been used.'

Forensic investigators sorted through the gore to establish, arguably, Australia's most gruesome time line of death.

'An examination of the blood stains, their differing characteristics and pattern of occurrence in various parts of the house, establish that Mr Price was first attacked by the prisoner in the principal bedroom of the premises,' Justice O'Keefe said. 'The wounds then inflicted were to the front of his body, and it is clear that thereafter he got off the bed after, or as, some further injuries were being inflicted on him in the course of his attempts to escape from his assailant, the prisoner. He escaped from the bedroom and moved down the hall in order to get outside the premises but was pursued by the prisoner, who stabbed him in the back a number of times.

'Whilst in the hallway he tried to switch on the light. At that time he was heavily blood-stained both front and back and appears to have then had further stab wounds inflicted to the front part of his body. In the course of his endeavour to escape, Mr Price reached the front door and opened it and, as is apparent from the blood stains on the outside knob of the front door, he succeeded in getting outside the house. However, he did not remain outside and was either dragged or, as is much less likely, came back into the house and fell in the hallway quite close to the open doorway that leads into the lounge room in which his body was later found by police.'

Police found Knight comatose on the floor. She was taken to hospital before being arrested. Knight claimed she knew nothing about the murder.

This is an extract from her interview with police on 4 March 2001 – three days after Price was found dead.

> Q: *Kathy, I'm investigating the death of John Price, known as 'Pricey' to a lot of people in Aberdeen, on or about Wednesday, the first of March. I have reason to believe that you may be the person responsible. Is there anything you can tell me about the matter?*
>
> A: *I don't know anything.*
>
> Q: *Can you recall the last thing that you remember?*
>
> A: *The last thing I remember was going out for tea with me daughter and the kids, coming home.*
>
> Q: *Do you recall going to Pricey's at all?*
>
> A: *I really don't know nothing.*
>
> Q: *Can you just take me to the last thing you actually recall, which is the Tuesday, 29th of February?*
>
> A: *The last thing I recall was, I don't know about your dates, but I went inside and watched a bit of TV.*
>
> Q: *Right, was Pricey there?*
>
> A: *M'mm.*
>
> Q: *Do you . . . can you tell me where he was?*
>
> A: *Not particularly.*
>
> Q: *And do you remember nothing after that?*
>
> A: *No.*

Fair dinkum? Nothing? No recollection at all?

'The prisoner claimed in her record of interview to have no recollection whatsoever of the events of and surrounding the death of Mr Price,' Justice O'Keefe said. 'The extent of her amnesia as claimed in her record of interview was virtually total, extending back into part of the day of 29 February 2000 and into 1 March 2000.

'However, she was able to remember and detail quite vividly events which appear to have immediately preceded Mr Price's death. Furthermore, on the morning after her admission to hospital she was able to give details of the medication she had taken and its quantity. Although this was before she was questioned by the police, she still claimed in the course of that questioning that she had no recollection of such events.

'Piecing these various strands of evidence together results in a picture in which her recollection ceases immediately before Mr Price's death and recommences after the skinning, dismemberment and partial cooking of Mr Price had taking place.

'This is not a credible pattern for a true amnesia, according to the psychiatric evidence which I accept. Moreover, during the time of which she claims to have no recollection, she performed a number of tasks that required a steady hand, the application of skill and an understanding of driving a motor vehicle and of operating an automatic teller machine. She also showered, changed her clothes and walked from her house back to Mr Price's house.'

Yep. The judge called bullshit on the whole 'I don't remember a thing' excuse.

'I do not believe the prisoner's statements as to her claimed amnesia,' Justice O'Keefe said. 'I am satisfied beyond reasonable doubt that she has much more recollection than she has claimed and that her claimed extent of amnesia is convenient for her, both emotionally and litigiously.

'Whether she remembers the events or not, they are horrendous. They were [also] premeditated. Even if she has no recollection of the actual killing, dismemberment and partial cooking of Mr Price, that may be regarded as no more than a blocking out by her of events that are so horrendous as to cause revulsion and rejection by her as the person responsible for such acts.'

'Katherine Mary Knight, you have pleaded guilty to and been convicted of the murder of John Charles Thomas Price at Aberdeen in the State of New South Wales on or about 29 February 2000,' Judge O'Keefe said when sentencing Knight. 'In respect of that crime I sentence you to imprisonment for life.'

Justice O'Keefe created history by handing out the first 'never to be released' sentence for a female. Knight was given 'life', without the possibility of parole. Knight, slammed as 'evil', changed her plea to guilty after originally claiming innocence.

'The prisoner has pleaded guilty to a murder which falls into the most serious category of murders,' O'Keefe said. 'I am satisfied beyond any doubt that such murder was premeditated. I am further satisfied in the same way that not only did she plan the murder, but she also enjoyed the horrific acts which followed in its wake as part of a ritual of death and defilement.

'The things which she did after the death of Mr Price indicate cognition, volition, calm and skill. I am satisfied beyond reasonable double that her evil actions were the playing out of her resentments arising out of her rejection by Mr Price, her impending expulsion from Mr Price's home and his refusal to share with her his assets, particularly his home, which he wanted to retain for his children.

'I have no doubt that her claim to amnesia forms part of her plan to affect madness in order to escape the consequences of her acts and to provide a convenient basis on which to rely to avoid detailed questioning by the police and escape punishment.

'The prisoner showed no mercy whatsoever to Mr Price. The last minutes of his life must have been a time of abject terror for him, as they were a time of utter enjoyment for her. At no time during the hearing or prior thereto did the prisoner express any regret for what she had done or any remorse for having done it; not even through the surrogacy of counsel.

'Her attitude in that regard is consistent with her general approach to the many acts of violence which she had engaged in against her various partners, namely *they deserved it.*

'In addition the prisoner's history of violence together with her flawed personality cause me to conclude, along with Dr Milton and the other psychiatrists called in the case, that she is without doubt a very dangerous person and likely, if released into the community, to commit further acts of serious violence, including even murder against those who cross her, particularly males. A crime of the kind committed by the prisoner calls for the maximum penalty the law empowers the court to impose.

'An examination of the cases referred to by counsel supports the view that I have formed, namely that the only appropriate penalty for the prisoner is life imprisonment and that parole should never be considered for her. The prisoner should never be released.'

Nanna

'Oh,' said Schembri after Knight gave her a blow-by-blow account of what she had (allegedly) done. 'But no. I still have never heard of you. I don't know a thing about that and, to be honest, that's your business.'

Knight stood in silence. Seconds passed, feeling like minutes to Schembri as she waited for the 'head' chef to respond. She didn't.

'So, did you do it?' Schembri blurted.

Fuck. Did I really just ask that? Schembri wished she could take it back. She thought about those prison movies again. *Yep. That's a no-no. They never go there.*

'Yes,' Knight said. 'I think I did.'

Schembri was now the silent one, happy to end the conversation there.

'But I don't know if I did or not,' Knight continued. 'I can't remember a thing. They say I did. And I can't argue with the evidence. But, honestly, I blacked out. It's all a complete blank.'

Schembri thought she better say something.

'And they gave you life?' she asked.

Knight stood proud. 'Not just life,' she said. 'Life without parole. I'm never getting out.'

Schembri served much of her four-year sentence locked down with Katherine Knight.

'She honestly doesn't remember killing him,' Schembri said. 'She told me that she only knows what they told her she did. And I believe her.'

Schembri has, for the first time ever, revealed how Katherine Knight spends her days locked away in Australia's most secure women's jail. The former model recounted a typical day for Knight, one that starts at 7 am every morning when she wakes to go to one of the most tedious jobs in prison.

'She makes headphones,' Schembri said. 'That's her job. She's stuck in a factory every day, from 8 am to 1 pm, making headphones on a big, loud machine.'

Knight is said to be one of the best workers in the head-phone factory and commands the top wage.

'She gets through more work than anyone,' Schembri said. 'She enjoys her job and takes pride in what she does. Four guards flank her. They watch her every move and are with her every day.'

After Knight finishes her day at the headphone factory, she eats lunch before retiring to her cell.

'Her cell is the same size as every other cell in the wing,' Schembri said. 'It's a one-out corner cell at the end of the wing. She has a bed, clothes, and the centrepiece of her room is a big old table that she uses for making art. She also sits at that table to write letters.'

Schembri described Knight as a hoarder whose cell is full of knitting, knick-knacks and art.

'Her room is very cluttered,' Schembri said. 'She had shit everywhere. She had been there for a long time, and it was like she'd kept everything she'd ever been given. Not many people ever got to go in her room. She keeps it very private. I was in there only once, to help her lift something she couldn't lift on her own. It was her private space. She crochets and has heaps of blankets and things she has made. There's wool piled everywhere. Lots of knitted things. She has tried to make it as homely and warm as possible. She's going to be there until she dies, so she has made it her home, a place she feels comfortable in.'

A corrections officer said jail hoarders like Knight are common. While men keep barren cells, women tend to keep anything and everything.

'They collect anything they ever get,' the officer said. 'To be honest, some of it is quite bizarre. In men's jails, inmates have very little in their cells, usually a couple of books, toiletries, maybe a magazine. In a women's jail, some will have 100 pens and 100 pencils stuck in a tin. Some of them keep empty chip packets. They'll fold them up neatly and press them down before stacking them into piles. One lady has a pile that is at least 200 packets high. They look like they've been ironed.

'Knight is one of those who has a very cluttered cell. She has shit stuck all over her walls, and blankets she has made are thrown over everything.'

Knight is also a prolific prison artist. She has become a skilled painter and raises money for the prison by selling her works.

'She's an incredible artist,' Schembri said. 'But she never signs anything she does – and never will. She doesn't want anyone making money off her name because she killed someone. She doesn't want some sick person buying her art because they think what she did was cool. The thought of someone hanging something on their wall just because she is a killer repulses her.

'She's amazing with pencil, paint and also pottery. A lot of her pottery is on display in the foyer at Mulawa. She has allowed them to sell a lot of it to raise money for charity and the jail – without her signature, of course.'

Schembri proudly displays a Knight artwork in her home.

'My son helped another kid in a visit with something, and Katherine saw it,' Schembri recalled. 'She thought it was beautiful and asked if she could do a painting for him to show she appreciated his kindness. She asked what he would like painted, and he said Bart Simpson. Katherine then went and did a beautiful portrait for him. I still have the painting at home. It is brilliant.'

Knight has little left for her outside of prison. Her family and friends have abandoned her.

'I never saw her on the phone,' Schembri said. 'I think all her friends and family have wiped her. I don't think she has anyone on the outside. I would say she has zero contact with the outside. Everyone would be on the phone every day, speaking to people outside, but I never saw that with Katherine. It was quite sad.'

But inside, in Mulawa Max, Knight is known as 'the Nanna'. She is arguably the most popular inmate in the prison. She is also a peacemaker.

'We called her the Nanna,' Schembri said. 'She is a gentle soul and not a criminal to me. She is a mediator at Mulawa. She's someone who sorted out problems before they got serious. She would pull the girls in and try to get them to sort out whatever it was before it ended up with someone going into segro [segregation] or getting more time added to their sentence.

'She would stop girls stealing from each other, and stop girls from fighting. But she never did it by standing over anyone. She never raised her hands to anyone. She was just someone who everyone loved.'

Knight is also the prison's event planner.

'She organises a big catch-up every Friday,' Schembri said. 'She organises all the food and makes sure that everyone in the wing is a part of it. She includes every single person, even those she doesn't really like. She does it to bring everyone together. It stops a lot of problems from happening.'

An active officer labelled Knight a prison 'boss'.

'She's the top boss of the jail,' the officer said. 'She takes no crap from anyone and absolutely gives it to the guards. If you come in to search her cell, she will stand in front of you with a smug face and scream at you. She will demand to watch you search the cell, and she will not leave the area. "No, I'm fuckin' staying here!" she'll scream. You have to use force to get rid of her, so we just leave her there and let her watch. It isn't worth the hassle. And every time you pick up something, she'll be like, "What are you touching that for?"'

The officer confirmed that Knight also plays the part of jailhouse mother.

'Yeah, they call her Nanna,' the officer said. 'She does the sewing and knitting for all the other ladies, and she plays the part. She also looks really old now. She hasn't aged well. In fact, she looks like a nanna. She is old with glasses and grey hair. She looks like your typical nan with the curly, old-school hair. She also wears cardigans.'

The officer described Knight's relationship with her fellow inmates.

'She is their confidante,' the officer said. 'They all go to her to talk and ask permission for whatever it is they want to do. She knows everything that goes on in the jail, and whatever she says goes.'

The officer explained that Knight is not your typical prison boss. She did not gain her position of authority by way of intimidation and violence.

'No, she has never raised her hands in prison,' the officer said. 'Not once. I think she has that level of respect because of her crime. Because she was so brutal. She has a lot of respect in the inmate population, that's for sure. They simply do not fuck around with her, and that's a fact.

'Most of the other heavies get respect for being tough. Other crims fear them. But Knight doesn't really have a record of violence while in jail. I would actually say she hasn't even had a single jail charge since she's been inside. Even the guards respect her a bit. She's the boss, put it that way. She would be the boss of any pod.'

So what's a boss?

'They sort out any problems in the pod,' the officer said. 'As a boss, Knight will be the one all the other inmates come to. If two girls are fighting, she'll step in and decide when and if it stops. She'll also give permission for them to fight. She would also arrange punishment.'

The officer said female jails, with head figures like 'Nanna', remain a throwback to a bygone prison era.

'That sort of thing doesn't exist in men's jails anymore,' the officer said. 'There is a much bigger hierarchy than in the male jails. It's a bit more like what it was like, say, in Long Bay back in the 70s. There are no real gangs in women's jails, and the female heavies are like the old-school male sweepers. The females are wired differently, and they are more like high school cliques than gangs.

'It is nothing like a male jail.'

Knight is housed in a section of Mulawa called 'Willet'. She is a Category 4 inmate – the highest and worst category a prisoner can be assigned – and always will be.

'She will never leave Mulawa,' said Schembri. 'She'll always be classified high-risk. She will never go to a place like Emu Plains, where she can see trees or walk in a field. She can never have a job mowing lawns or where she can leave the jail. She will always be locked in a factory because everyone thinks she's a heartless, callous monster. But she has emotions. I've seen them. I've seen her cry. She is no monster, but she'll always be caged like one.'

Knight is a rare breed of prisoner; her crime has determined how she will live the rest of her life. While other murderers can earn privileges, Knight cannot. She will forever be kept in a maximum-security prison.

'There would be such an uproar in the media if she was ever reclassified,' said prison activist and former inmate Kat Armstrong, who served time with Knight. 'It doesn't matter how well she behaves; despite the fact that what goes on in prison has nothing to do with the public, it's the public who decides how she lives. The Alan Joneses and the Ray Hadleys [popular Sydney radio hosts] of the world will make sure she has the toughest life possible. People like those two want to know she is being punished in the worst possible way, despite her behaviour while inside. It doesn't matter that she has been a model prisoner all this time. She is treated like a child killer. And she has victims – the children of the man she killed. If she was moved to another prison or had her classo [classification] changed, they would be notified and there would be an uproar. That's why she will always be treated as the worst of the worse.

'She is so well behaved that she's the general manager's clerk, for god's sake. She has the most trusted position in the jail.'

Most prisoners are rewarded and punished based on their behaviour. An incentive system encourages them to behave. Be good and you will get a reward. Knight's only incentive to behave is to avoid punishment. There is a stick . . . but there will never be a carrot.

'No, there's no incentive for her to behave,' Armstrong said. 'She will never be paroled; she will never be reclassified. Her only incentive to behave is to make her own time easier by being a model prisoner. By being a model prisoner, she is left alone and allowed to do her art. If she mucked up and carried on, then they would take things away from her and make her life as difficult as possible.'

Still, Knight is widely regarded as a model inmate, liked by all ... even the officers.

'I was there when she first came in,' Armstrong said. 'Me and some other long-termers sat her down and explained some things. We tried to mentor her on the best way for her to do her jail time. We told her not to think about next year or the year after. We told her not to think about getting out. We told her to just live day by day and do what you can. It was about being polite, not getting in other people's dramas and basically keeping your head down. We also told her to take up anything that was available to her that she might enjoy, and for her that was art and pottery. She has done copious amounts of pottery and artwork over the years.

'She still has a lot of contact with those long-termers and often receives letters from people she was in jail with.'

Armstrong has called for Knight to be rewarded for her behaviour. While she will not argue against the killer's life sentence, she does believe Knight has earned the right to enjoy better living conditions.

'It is outrageous that she can never be reclassified,' Armstrong said. 'By now she should be in a camp. She should be in a place like Emu Plains or Parramatta Transitional Centre, where she could actually do something constructive and productive with her time, not just for herself but also for other people. But because of Ivan Milat and the Ebony Simpson killer, who come under the 'serious offenders' category, she will never get that opportunity. She has been classified with the likes of them and has no prospects of being reclassified or moving through the system. It is legislation, and it would take something extraordinary to have it changed. For the good running and order of the jail, it would be beneficial for people like Katherine to have access to education and programs, which they can't get now. Doing something in the jail, like mowing the lawns, would be helpful and productive and not affect anyone in society. But they don't care about the prisoners' welfare. They just want them locked up in maximum-security on heavy drugs. It's no existence.'

And it is difficult to argue as long as nobody is ever put at risk. Not one woman who we spoke to described Knight as violent or a threat. Here's what another one of Mulawa's residents, who asked to remain anonymous, had to say about the woman who butchered her boyfriend:

'Oh, she was rough as guts . . . but I don't know. There was something about her. She was very artistic. Very caring. She was not what you expected. She was doing all these drawings of Snow White while I was in there. She got an easy time in there. She got it much easier than what Lucy Dudko did.

'Knight was working in the laundry while I was in. And she was good to us. She would always be slipping us extra blankets and looking after us. She was really good. I don't have a bad word to say about her. I know she's portrayed as an evil woman, but she has never been that way to me, or anyone I know. She had no aggression, and I was more than happy to live with her. She wouldn't hurt a fly.'

You can bet that would be argued by those affected by her horrendous crime.

I Might Kill Again

Knight began to shake, first her hands and then her head.

'No,' she said softly.

Louder now. '*No.*'

And finally she screamed, her desperation filling the entire wing. '*Noooo!*'

The prison officer stood, completely calm.

'Look,' he said. 'It's not ideal but that's just the way it is. It won't be forever but right now there just aren't enough beds, and the only solution is for people like you to go two-out. You are going to have to share a cell. Don't worry, we'll make sure it's with someone you like.'

Knight was now white. 'You can't put someone in with me – you just can't!'

The officer raised his hands. 'Why not? Not everyone can go one-out.'

Knight deadpanned the guard.

'Because I might kill her,' she said.

Knight has never admitted to her crime, but she recently confessed she's capable of murder when she refused to share a cell with another prisoner.

'The jail was getting really full, and they were talking about putting her in a two-out cell,' Schembri recalled. 'And she freaked out. I had never seen her get emotional or animated, and she had to plead with the officers. She told them that she was scared. And she was. She was scared that she might have an episode and kill someone else. I spoke to her about it, and it was the only time I ever saw fear in her eyes. She was genuinely worried that she might kill someone again and not even know she had done it.'

Schembri, largely because of the deep anxiety she saw in Knight's eyes when she talked to her about her fear of killing an anonymous cellmate, believes that the head-chopping, bum-cooking murderer has no recollection of her crime.

'She knew what she had done but didn't remember doing it,' Schembri said. 'She was worried that whatever was in her would come out again. She said she had something inside of her that wasn't right, but she didn't know what. And you can only believe her. She's in for life and will never get out. She doesn't claim to be innocent and has nothing to gain by saying that. She had read everything she'd done and was heartbroken over it.'

Schembri claimed Knight often got upset over how she was perceived by the public. Knight had access to newspapers and magazines detailing her crimes.

'She knew what everyone thought about her,' Schembri said. 'And to know she was thought of as a monster, well . . . it broke her heart. She is nothing like the person that she is portrayed to be. The Katherine Knight I know has values, morals, beliefs and is a deeply caring person.'

Schembri spoke to Knight on several occasions about the night she butchered her boyfriend. Knight claims the man she killed had been sexually assaulting a child.

'She told me she does remember finding out that he had been touching up a young family member,' Schembri said. 'She says that must be what motivated her to do it. She thinks that's what made her snap, because there is only one thing that she won't stand for and that's abusing a child.

'She also told me she'd been in a violent, aggressive relationship and had been the victim of violence. But that had never set her off. It was molestation [of her child] that had sent her over the edge. She was very honest and open about everything in her life. It was just the murder that was a complete blank.'

And does the monster regret the killing and the cooking?

'She was remorseful,' Schembri said. 'She didn't remember killing him, but she wishes she hadn't done it. She has ruined her family. And she has ruined her life.'

Lucy Dudko
Cuffs and Chains

Lucy slowly, calmly and complicitly walked into her cell.

'Lockdown!' screamed the red-faced officer, sweat pouring down his brow. 'Move it. NOW!'

Lucy attempted to block out the noise – the sirens, the shouts and the screams. She hummed a tune as she buried her head into her pillow, oblivious to the girls running past her cell and the guards occasionally pushing – or pulling – them.

Lucy the librarian, mild and well mannered, did not care for the chaos. This was not the mousey blonde's problem.

But it soon would be . . .

'Male in the wing,' came the booming cry.

Thump!

Whoever was shouting was now thumping on her door.

Thump!

The rattle of a key. The lock snapping back.

What? Why are they coming in here? Why me?

The prison had been quiet for hours. The hysteria had continued for a while after the girls were sent to their cells, but, tightly locked down and nothing to do, boredom soon took over. Most of them napped now.

Lucy put down her book to confront the officer, the meathead now standing in her cell.

'Lucy Dudko,' the officer said. 'Let's go.'

Lucy did not move an inch.

'Me?' she asked, genuinely surprised, though she shouldn't have been. *She should have learned by now.* 'Why? I haven't done anything.'

The officer shook his head and smiled. 'Really?' he said. 'Well, we'll just have to see about that, hey?'

Soon little lady Lucy was shuffling down the wing in chains.

What had she done? Nothing. *Did the officers know she was innocent?* Probably. *But did they care?* No. Two women had just escaped Berrima Correctional Centre, fleeing through a hole in a wall. And what do you do when there is an escape in a prison where the woman who pulled off the world's most famous jailbreak is held?

Well, you interrogate her of course. Chain her, charge her and put her in solitary confinement.

This is the story of how a little lady called Lucy Dudko – a model inmate, by all accounts – did her prison time. It is a story of cell searches and cuffs. Of solitary confinement and stolen mail.

'When I first went into maximum [security] at Mulawa, I became mates with Lucy,' said a former prisoner who spoke under the condition of anonymity. 'She became my best mate. I was young, 19, and she took me under her wing. She was such a nice lady and someone who never did a thing wrong. But, geez, did they give her a hard time. They were always into her. She was always getting her room ramped [searched], and they were taking things from her and smashing stuff.

'They ended up separating us too. Not because we were causing trouble or anything like that. They did it just to punish Lucy. They wanted to keep her isolated, and they didn't want her getting close to anyone.

'She spent a lot of time in segro. It really fucked her up. I think it was about three months, from what I recall. And I know it really messed with her. She hallucinated while she was in there. She used to see spiders and stuff like that. It sent her crazy. It almost broke her.

'They made her do her time hard, not because of how she acted in jail but because of what she'd done to get there.'

So, what did she do?

Oh, come on. *Surely you know?*

Jailbreak

Dudko handed the helicopter pilot the cash – four crisp one-hundred-dollar notes.

'Now, can you take me to see the stadium?' she asked.

The pilot looked at the pretty blonde with the thick Russian accent and nodded. *Another tourist wanting to see the Olympic stadium. Easy money.*

'Sure,' he said. 'Not a problem.'

Tim Joyce had spent most of 1999 hovering over Homebush in Western Sydney, chatting to Japanese, German and English tourists as they took pictures of Sydney Olympic Park ahead of the 2000 Olympic Games. His three-seater Bell helicopter had become very familiar with the short trip from Bankstown Airport to the venue.

So he took Lucy's money, made his ascent and headed off to the west.

Joyce used a two-way radio headset to speak to the shy tourist sitting by his side.

'There it is,' he said as he pointed to the newly built 110,000-seat stadium, the biggest sporting structure in the world at the time. 'That's where it's all going to happen.'

Lucy didn't seem interested, the little lady looking off to her left. *Daydreaming, maybe?*

'Oh,' she said. 'Fine.'

Joyce pushed on.

'And that's the village,' he said. 'Where all the athletes will stay. Impressive, right?'

'Uh?' Lucy said. 'Oh. Yes. Right.'

Lucy was clearly somewhere else.

'Is that the prison?' she asked, pointing out towards Silverwater, a stone's throw away from Sydney Olympic Park.

Joyce nodded at the woman, happy she had suddenly found her spark. He met her enthusiasm with a lashing of his own.

'Yes, indeed,' he said. 'That's what they call the MRRC. It is a maximum-security jail. That's where everyone goes when they are first sentenced. Scary-looking place, hey?'

Lucy, suddenly attentive, turned to look the pilot straight in the eye.

'Wow,' she said. 'Could we take a look at that?'

This was not an unusual request. *Who wasn't interested in prisons?*

'Sure,' he said.

Lucy beamed as he tracked off to the left, the prison looming large.

'That's one of the yards,' he said. 'Look closely and you might see a murderer or two.'

How about a bank robber?

Lucy was a picture of concentration. 'Can we go lower?' she asked. 'I can't see.'

Joyce shook his head. 'No can do. That's restricted airspace. We can't go flying into a prison. Time to head back.'

Joyce peered to his right, plotting his course home. And that's when he saw the gun.

Oh, fuck!

'This is a hijack!' the blonde shouted. 'You will land in the prison.'

Lucy pointed the pistol at his head.

Maybe it's a toy? Where would she get a gun?

Joyce considered overpowering the woman who, until now, seemed tiny and timid. Well, to be truthful, the only thing intimidating about her was the gun. He looked at it again, wondering whether or not it could be a replica.

Shit! What do I know about guns? Maybe it is real?

'Not a problem,' he said. 'Look, don't worry, she'll be right. I'll do whatever you want.'

Joyce was an experienced pilot. He had been trained to deal with scenarios just like this one. He reached towards the control panel, his finger hovering over an unmarked button. One press would activate a silent alarm that would alert authorities of a hijacking in progress.

'NO!' Lucy shouted before jamming the barrel of the gun into the side of his head. 'No alarms.'

Proving to Joyce that she was not only serious but also well prepared, she ripped off his headset so he had no way to communicate.

The pilot began his descent. Next stop: the Metropolitan Remand and Reception Centre.

Thwat! Thwat! Thwat!

Three bullets were fired as the prisoner pulled himself into the cockpit.

'John,' Lucy cried before handing him the gun. The inmate looked down at the weapon. It was no replica. It was a fully loaded Ruger pistol. And now it was in the hands of an infamous bank robber, one who was awaiting trial for shooting at a police officer.

'Get us out of here!' the man, clad in prison-issue green, screamed as he waved the gun.

Joyce had no doubt that the prisoner knew how to use the piece of metal he was holding. And he had no doubt he would use it, too, unless the pilot did exactly what he said. But right now the hijacker was more worried about the prison guards – the ones who were shooting high-calibre bullets from high-powered rifles. The first bullet hit the landing skid, the second hit dirt and the third almost ripped through a steering cable.

Fuck this. I'm out of here.

The biggest threat was no longer the inmate waving the gun.

I'll deal with him later.

Joyce pulled the throttle and the helicopter thundered into the sky.

Soon the inmate – well, the *former* inmate – was waving the gun. Again.

He pointed. 'See that big green patch of land? I want you to land there.'

Joyce nodded. 'Yep,' he said. 'I can do that.'

The helicopter blades churned up grass as the Bell touched down at a North Ryde oval called Christie Park.

'Switch it off,' the gunman ordered. Joyce did what he was told.

'You're coming with us!' Lucy screamed at Joyce over the slowing rotor blades. 'Get out.'

The gunman turned to the woman who had just orchestrated Australia's most daring prison escape. 'No,' he said. 'We don't want a hostage. That will get us another ten years. I'll tie him up.'

And so he did, and soon Lucy Dudko and the gunman were gone.

She had done it. Lucy had hijacked a helicopter and broken her lover free from one of Australia's most secure prisons. She was a modern-day Bonnie on the run with her Clyde.

Lucy Dudko had visited John Reginald Killick at least 20 times at the MRRC before breaking him out of prison in what would become one of the world's most famous jailbreaks.

Killick, Dudko's lover of four years, was incarcerated on remand in the Silverwater maximum-security jail, awaiting three trials in three courts – the most serious at Wollongong District Court, where he would face up to two charges of armed robbery and one of shooting with intent to kill.

'Lucy was adamant she was going to get me out,' said Killick. 'She came in and visited me all the time. She was an absolute mess. She was terrified of being without me because she was having problems with her ex-husband. They were going through a nasty break-up and she needed me to protect her. She was in the middle of a big custody battle for her child. There were threats and she was under immense pressure. She was getting anonymous phone calls with people speaking Russian and calling her a bitch.'

Dudko and Killick had been inseparable since meeting at a party in Canberra in 1995.

Killick had spent most of his adult life in jail, having served sentences for armed robbery and related offences in New South Wales, Queensland and Victoria.

'She became dependent on me,' Killick said. 'And she couldn't cope when I was arrested and sent back to jail. She was terrified to be without me.'

And so she decided she was going to break her lover out.

'She couldn't cope with me inside and she saw no other way,' Killick said. 'She was alone and needed me. She wrote me letters every single day and visited me every other. She talked about getting me out during every visit, and we started speaking about how it could be done.'

But Killick's history made it almost impossible . . .

'I had little hope of escaping,' Killick said. 'I was classified "extreme high-risk" because I'd escaped from a couple of jails over the years and also had a couple of other failed attempts.

'I was escorted by armed guards to all my court visits,' Killick said. 'That ruled out trying to escape when going off to court, which is the easiest way. I told Lucy that they were on to me and I couldn't do a runner. I thought going to the prison hospital was probably the only chance. We had all these conversations about how we might do it by the hospital, but even that seemed like a million-to-one shot. I had more of a chance of digging my way out with a spoon.'

Killick told Dudko to forget about him. He wasn't getting out. 'And then I met this guy who was a helicopter pilot. And he said he could get me out. There were 20 wings in Silverwater, and out of all of them, I end up with this pilot who told me it could be done.'

Lucy smiled when Killick gave her the news.

'I think this can be done,' he said during a visit. 'I think you can get me out. There is this guy in here who says he'll do it for 20 K. I think he's a con-man, but I reckon we can get all the information about how to do it ourselves if we give him a bit of cash. And then we can do the rest.'

So Lucy put some money in the 'con-man's' account.

'And then he told us everything about heights, speeds and times,' Killick said. 'But the most important piece of information he gave us was about the emergency transponder. If he hadn't told us that, we would have been screwed.'

Lucy was in.

'She thought it was a great idea and that it would work,' Killick said. 'The only thing I had to do was be out on the oval at that particular time. She did a trial run and was happy with everything, so she planned it all and told me when.'

And Lucy got Killick out. But their freedom was short-lived . . .

'Just one night, please,' Lucy said before paying $62 in cash. It was 2 pm on Friday, 7 May 1999.

ID?

'No, sorry. Don't have any,' she said, looking down at the check-in form. 'I lost my purse and haven't got my cards back yet.'

Lucy, pen in hand, began scribbling on the sheet: *Name of Occupants?* Mr and Mrs M. G. Brown. *Address?* 1/11 Second Avenue, Merrylands.

The manager of the Bass Hill Tourist Park in south-west Sydney, Phillip Taylor, suspected the woman was being sneaky.

Probably just another married woman having an affair . . .

Lucy was no longer blonde, her hair now bob-length and black.

Taylor handed her a key. 'Cabin 14. Enjoy your stay.'

Killick was not seen until dusk, when Taylor witnessed a man arguing with a taxi driver before entering her cabin.

Yep. Certainly an affair.

And it was. But Mr and Mrs M. G. Brown weren't sneaking from spouses, they were hiding from the cops.

'Surrender!' the heavily armed officer screamed, the loud-speaker turning his already booming voice into a fearsome roar. 'Come out slowly, with your hands in the air.'

Stunned tourists and residents at the Bass Hill Tourist Park, rudely awoken in the middle of the night, began peeking out windows and barely cracked doors. What they saw was simply frightening: bulletproof vests and polycarbonate riot shields, floodlights and the roaming red dots of laser-sighted rifles.

The general continued to shout: 'Mr John Killick and Mrs Lucy Dudko, we have a warrant for your arrest. Come out now.'

The boss was flanked by an army from the State Protection Group (SPG). The most lethal and highly trained members of the NSW police force were armed with tactical shotguns, M16 semi-automatic rifles and UMP subma-chine guns equipped with flashlights, laser sights and a full magazine of .45-calibre bullets that could be fired at the rate of 700 rounds per minute.

The weapons were all drawn and aimed at Cabin 14. There would be no miraculous escape this time. Killick and Dudko had just two options: *surrender or die.*

With more than a dozen SPG officers about to bang down his door, Killick surrendered, walking out of the cabin at 2.30 am wearing blue shorts, a red shirt and thongs.

'Hands up!' the boss yelled, and Killick complied. 'Walk forward until I tell you to stop.'

Killick was ordered to lie face-down on the asphalt near the entrance to the park. Then the SPG pounced. He was soon cuffed, shackled and in the back of an armoured van.

Lucy Dudko – aka Mrs Brown – walked out five minutes later, arms raised, wearing jeans and a T-shirt. She was cuffed and collared without incident. After 46 days on the run, they were done. Busted. Police entered the cabin and confiscated everything they owned: two overnight bags half-filled with clothes. *Oh, and a Luger semi-automatic pistol and a double-barrelled replica Derringer.*

The police had located the most wanted couple in Australia, and now Killick was going back to jail. And Lucy? Well, she was going there too – but for her it was a first. And she wasn't going to like it one bit. Now, let's get back to the cuffs and chains. The solitary cells and stolen mail. And the punishment for the prison escape Lucy – this time – had nothing to do with.

Paying the Price

Lucy Dudko sat silently in the back of the prison truck. She looked down at the chains dangling from her wrists.

Why? she thought. *What have I done?*

Lucy had been a perfect inmate ever since she was taken into custody. She had not complained about stints in solitary confinement; about being guarded by at least two officers every time she was taken from her cell; or about having her cells ramped every other week, the intruders throwing everything she owned to the floor.

But, after five years of harassment, she thought she was past all that. Sentenced to a maximum of ten years for her role in busting her older lover from jail, Dudko had spent the first years of her sentence at the notoriously harsh Mulawa women's prison in western Sydney. Subsequently, she was moved to the far more prisoner-friendly Berrima Correctional Centre, located in the picturesque Southern Highlands, halfway between Sydney and Canberra.

She had enjoyed her time so far at Berrima, a jail catering for prisoners classed from minimum- to medium-risk. Lucy had a good job in the printing room and had been allowed to regularly visit the library to indulge her passion for books.

But now she was stuck in the back of a prison truck on a two-hour trip, chains rattling and sweat pouring down her brow. She had no idea where she was being taken, let alone why. She was soon put out of her misery. Well, to be more accurate, she was soon made miserable.

'Out,' the officer demanded as he opened the truck door. 'We're here.'

But where is 'here'?

'Home, of course,' said the officer.

Lucy was blinded by the light of the midday sun on her face as she was dragged from the truck. But her eyes eventually adjusted to the glare.

Oh no. Not here . . .

Lucy had been taken back to Mulawa. She was escorted past the gates and put through the drill she knew way too well – the searches, the X-rays and the march down the wing to her new cell.

'Not this one,' she said as the officer opened the heavy door. 'You can't put me in solitary. I've done nothing wrong. Why are you putting me in here?'

The officer said nothing, merely grunted as he locked the door. Lucy was kept in solitary confinement for five days. She did not know why she was in or when she was going to be let out. She would later learn that she was being punished only because of her original crime. Because of who she was and what she had done . . . at least before she was sentenced.

'She was at Berrima and two girls escaped,' Killick said. 'Lucy had nothing to do with it, but they grabbed her and put her in a van because of *who* she was. She was a model prisoner, but they shoved her in a van and took her down to Mulawa. And they put her in segro for no other reason than the fact she was Lucy.'

Dudko barely knew the two girls who'd escaped from Berrima Jail in October 1999. She'd worked in the same print shop – a minimum-security section of the jail – that they'd made their getaway from. But she had never said more than hello to the pair who would climb through a hole in a wall before being apprehended in Darlinghurst, Sydney.

'That was the only link that Lucy had to this pair,' Killick said. 'That she had worked in the same building as them. And for that they moved her back to the worst jail for women. And they put her in solitary and left her in there for five days.

'Her property also went missing when they moved her. All your property is moved when you are moved, and she never got it back. She complained and it even went as far as the ombudsman, but the bottom line is that they didn't do anything about it.'

Killick alleges that Dudko was moved because of the crime she had committed, not the risk she posed.

'That was all it was,' Killick said. 'Two girls had escaped, and they couldn't have the embarrassment of having the woman responsible for the most famous escape in Australian history kept in there.'

Killick, a three-time escapee, said his former lover was not a flight risk. He claims her elaborate helicopter plan was a one-time deal.

'She did her time hard because they wouldn't put her through the classification system like everyone else,' Killick said. 'She had never been in any trouble in her life aside from her crime. She wasn't going to escape. She should have progressed. Even when she got to minimum security, she wrote to me and said that she was emptying the garbage with another girl. She went to step outside the gate at Dillwynia and a screw stopped her. She told him she was a minimum-security inmate and just doing her job. The guard said it didn't matter. He said she was Lucy Dudko, and if she ran off he would lose his job. She was a very high-profile inmate, and they treated her as such. She never got any type of external leave or privileges because they were worried about her escaping. She missed out on a lot of the basic rights other inmates got. When she went to hospital she was escorted by at least two officers. She would be taken in a belt and all that, like she was some kind of monster.

'They had a thing with Lucy and handcuffs. They would put them on her whenever they took her anywhere. She was considered Australia's highest risk female inmate. She was always the highest category and never left alone. She was always in a two-out or three-out cell. They didn't take their eyes off her. And I have no doubt they roughed her up a bit from time to time, but they would have believed they were just doing their jobs.'

Lucy never made an official complaint about the cell raid. About the pain and the torture. She penned a statement about being locked up in Mulawa in 2004. Her move back to the infamous women's jail broke her completely. Finally, she felt compelled to complain. But she never sent the statement . . .

'Nothing happened with that stat declaration,' Killick continued. 'It was a [specialist] squad that had come in. They had come in from Long Bay, and they tipped up a couple of the wings [looking for contraband]. She was singled out, and that was just something she was used to because of who she was. That was part of her life inside. I think at this point she was just fed up with it all.'

And Lucy didn't want to go back to solitary – the place that had her 'seeing spiders' and almost 'going over the edge'.

'She did it tough when she first went in,' Killick said. 'She hadn't even been in trouble before, let alone been to jail, so it was always going to be a shock. But there is no way anyone could have expected what was coming her way.

'They put her straight into an observation cell. They had two cameras in there, watching her the whole time, and she was kept in there for three months. They didn't even let her have a shower curtain. She was on her own, but she was being watched the entire time.'

Killick said the Department of Corrections justified the use of an observation cell by claiming that Lucy was suicidal.

'Well, that's what they said,' Killick continued. 'The excuse they used to keep her there. But, no, she wasn't suicidal. Not at all.'

Lucy spent the first three months of her prison sentence locked in solitary confinement for up to 23 hours a day. She wasn't suicidal when she went in, but she claims the stint in the observation cell left her with lifelong mental health problems.

'They would only bring her out for an hour a day to walk in the kitchen,' Killick said. 'They would let her go for a stride around there, and that was the only time she got out during her first three months in jail.'

Killick claims the three-month stint in solitary was a warning to others: don't embarrass the system . . . or else!

'She had embarrassed the system. This was their payback. She wasn't a risk to herself or anyone else. And she was never going to escape. So you tell me another reason for why they did it.'

Lucy was taken out of the observation cell after three months. She would soon wish she was back on her own, 'spiders' and all . . .

*

Lucy stormed towards the obese woman who had issued the latest threat to Kipling's new resident. The fat lady sat still, partly because she was in shock to see the meek woman finally reacting and partly because she was too heavy to move.

'That's enough from you,' Dudko said in a stern yet measured tone as she bent down and grabbed a chair leg with each hand. 'I will not listen to anything from someone as disgusting as you.'

Whack!

The beast toppled down and smacked onto the ground after the diminutive former librarian showed the strength of a construction worker to lift the chair.

'Leave me alone, or it will get worse,' Lucy threatened. 'You make me sick.'

The fat lady, sprawled out on the concrete, struggling like a whale stranded on the beach, said nothing.

'It is the only incident of violence I am aware of,' said Killick. 'She never lashed out at anyone other than this woman, and that was only because she was a child killer. After they took Lucy out of solitary they put her in a wing full of sickos. They were mostly child killers, and she couldn't stand them. They used to give her heaps because she was nothing like them. Anyway, one day she just got fed up. One of the child killers had a go at Lucy, and she ran up, pulled her chair out and tipped her onto the ground. She was a big, fat thing and went down pretty hard. She went on her arse, and that was the end of it. I was pretty proud of Lucy when I found out about it.'

So the first-time offender, a woman who broke her lover out of prison, was locked up with child killers?

'Yes, they put her in a place called Kipling,' Killick said. 'And that is an absolutely horrible place mostly used to house baby killers. It's a wing in Mulawa that they use for strict protections. It's a place for people who are so sick that they need to be protected from other inmates because of their crimes.

'There was absolutely no need for it, and she hated it. She despised anyone who had committed crimes against children, but they locked her up with that class of criminal because they just didn't know what to do with her.'

Lucy even had to share a cell with a woman who had harmed a child.

'At all times she had to be in a two-out cell,' Killick said. 'They didn't want her being on her own, plotting an escape. And if her cellmate had to go out overnight to attend a court appearance or something like that, then they would put her in a three-out cell. She was sharing cells with child killers and it was a nightmare.

'She became frustrated because she just couldn't understand why she was in there with them. She was a mother and she despised them and everything they stood for. A lot of them had very light sentences because they were considered mentally unstable. It was a pretty bad time for her.'

Eventually, Dudko's relentless requests to be moved out of the protection wing were heard. She was moved to a maximum-security general population wing at Mulawa. And she went from being the enemy of a child killer to the friend of a husband killer.

'She became good friends with Katherine Knight,' Killick said of the never-to-be-released prisoner you recently met. 'She said that [Knight] took her under her wing and looked after her. She said she really liked Katherine.'

Dudko soon settled into a routine. She kept her head down and avoided trouble.

'She ended up with a lot of friends,' Killick said. 'She was well respected in the prison system. She wasn't into drugs and stayed out of all that type of business.'

Lucy spent much of her time with her head buried in a book.

'She spent most of her time studying law,' Killick said. 'She would go to the library and research anything she could that would help build an appeals case for both me and herself. She sent me lots of cases that she'd found and photocopied in the library in a bid to help me. She found cases suitable for me because I was doing my own High Court appeal. She was also doing her own, and she did a pretty good job of it. We had to because we couldn't get Legal Aid to help.'

Lucy also liked to spend time in the prison garden.

'She eventually got a job in the gardens, and she really enjoyed it,' Killick said. 'She was a good worker wherever she went, and I think the screws even ended up having a begrudging respect for her. As I said, she never touched drugs and had no intention of escaping, so they began to respect her. She also had a wicked sense of humour.'

Lost Letters and Lost Love

No. 1955, 16/11/04

Hi Boy!

That Lucy and John story (the Emu Plains version). Lucy had this young stud, John Killick, 15 years younger than her. So she got him out and was sentenced to 12–15 years. But the rumour is the young stud is out, and he left her because she is too old and her sentence is too long. The stud couldn't wait until the end. I think we could publish an entire book 'Myths and Legends of the John and Lucy Story', as a second volume to the real story. Can you believe it?

Anyway, today I went to this induction course again. This time we had education officers telling us about their places, programs and service managers too. They are telling us most of the programs won't start until after xmas. Most of the people in the course will be out in two months anyway. But I still have 18 months to go, so I will try. They also said they are going to employ a lot of staff. The horticulture teacher will probably start after xmas, so my ideas about the nature place and the nursery will be back on the agenda. Yesterday the program manager said that the idea is really good. I'd love to work with plants in or out. Maybe I will manage to get a good job too. We will see. I also called the classo lady today to find out about my lost property and she said that the shop is open again, so maybe my stuff will come back? As for my cards . . . I don't know. Someone was going to find out about them at Berrima too. I asked her about my classo. She said at Berrima I was C2, but because of the penalty I am C3 at Dillwynia. I told her about my situation and she said that tomorrow they are having a meeting and they will talk about me. We will see. I also asked about moving to a low-needs jail. She said I needed to be in medium. Rang Gloria. She had an absolutely marvellous holiday! The weather was good and she enjoyed the stay greatly. And no problem with the accommodation; very cheap and comfortable.

Got three letters from you! 2011, 12 and 13. 2011 on one envelope and the other two in another with clippings. I am glad you are reasonable. I can't figure out in your letter if you were booked for a phone call to the chamber magistrate? In letters 2012 and 2013 nothing is said about this. So what happened? Let me know please. I am trying to establish a law library in Dillwynia. It is very hard because all the necessary books are periodic issues, like the law report, criminal reports and Commonwealth reports. They are very expensive. But I pointed out the MRRC library could have extra copies. But I think I won't be able to help you because only God knows when this plan eventuates, if it eventuates at all. It's funny that you wrote about your premonition seven years ago of what happens now! But can you imagine that one?

Lucy and Alex in 1983.

Lucy: Oh Gosh. I just had a vision.

Alex: What?

Lucy: I just had a vision of what will happen in 2004!

Alex: Well, I know what will happen. I will be a famous scientist and I will have 10 lovers.

Lucy: Will you be living in Russia?

Alex: Of course. What else, stupid?

Lucy: Well, I'll be in Australia, we will be divorced, and I will be in love with a bank robber. All will be informed about this love. You will be teaching English and collecting the Australian dole. And you will be known only as the ex-husband of Lucy Dudko, due to a helicopter escape.

Can you imagine his reaction? Ha-ha-ha.

Love you,

Lucy

*The last letter was written on 10/11/04.

They lost about 1000 of your letters!!!!

Lucy Dudko also wrote letters – a staggering 4500 in just six years. This one was exclusively obtained for this book, in which she speaks about her lost property and harsh treatment. It also shows the 'wicked' sense of humour described by Killick.

This letter was delivered and received. Many were not. Killick claims more than 1000 letters written by Lucy or to Lucy were stolen by prison officials intent on punishing the high-profile lovebirds.

'When we first got arrested, I told her that I would write to her every day,' Killick said. 'I was concerned that they might intercept our mail, so I said that we should number our letters so we knew what got through and what they had taken. The first letter was number one, and so on. So we knew when they were taking letters. If you got a letter numbered 226, and the next one you got was numbered

228 . . . well, then you knew they had taken 227. I didn't miss a day. I wrote a letter every day I was in jail, and she would have only missed a hundred or so. We sent each other thousands and thousands of letters. I still have most of the ones they didn't take.

'A whole box was never returned to her,' Killick said. 'She was furious about it, but there was nothing she could do. But at least she had the opportunity to read those ones. The ones they took before she got them, well, that hurt more.

'And I think they did it just to be cruel. Some of the people in prison only ever got two letters in their whole life. A lot of people in the prison system resented us. There were some bastards who didn't like us. I think it came from up top because of our crimes. There were always letters missing – and the more we complained, the more that went missing.'

Lucy was released from prison on 8 May 2006. She served exactly seven years of her maximum ten-year sentence.

John Killick and Lucy Dudko are now estranged. Despite the thousands of love letters and a request to be married in 2000 while in jail – a request that was denied – the Bonnie and Clyde of Australian crime have not seen each other since they were captured in 1999.

'She doesn't want anything to do with me,' he said. 'She's moved on. I've spoken to her, but she said it's too painful. I have to respect that.'

Killick recalled the moment a minister visited him in prison to tell him Dudko was ending her relationship with him.

'It was in 2005,' Killick said. 'A year before she got out. She sent a minister to come and see me in jail, and he said Lucy had rediscovered her faith. I told him I didn't buy most of that stuff in the Bible. Two weeks later, I was told the relationship was over.'

Matters were complicated even further when Killick was released from prison in 2015. As part of his parole conditions, Killick was banned from contacting Dudko until September 2022.

'We both served our time,' Killick said of the NSW parole board's decision. 'My risk of reoffending was assessed as being one out of 22 – the lowest possible mark. This isn't about Lucy and me being a threat to society the moment we catch up for coffee; this is about revenge. For what happened in that prison yard . . . for embarrassing them.'

Killick revealed that he has reached out to his former lover.

'Legally, I can't see her . . . I need her permission,' Killick said. 'But I spoke to her; she was pretty receptive. But then she had a change of heart, and I think some people got in her ear. I had her number and then she changed it. She said she would only get in trouble seeing me and that she needed to leave it behind.

'She wants to leave it all in the past; the memories are too painful. I was hoping we would be friends. I don't know about a love reunion, but I certainly wanted to have some sort of relationship with her. I know she's very strong in the church and that she has been back to Russia. I know she is still very stressed.'

Lucy – or 'Red Lucy', as she was dubbed by the press – was officially described as a model inmate who performed 'maintenance and garden work' at the Dillwynia Correctional Centre. She also completed a desktop publishing course when she was released.

She is now living with God . . . and without John. She has changed her name and is now living on the North Coast of New South Wales in a tightly knit church-going community.

Belinda Van Krevel
The Brunette and Her Body

He slammed the heavy, reinforced steel door.

'That will wake up a few of them,' the male officer said.

'Yeah, mate,' came the reply from an equally burly man. 'We don't want any surprises. Let's make sure they all know we're here.'

He nodded to his squad of four – a scrum of muscle and might, all specially trained for prison's most violent and dangerous work.

'Male in the wing,' he cried. 'Male squad in the wing.'

Still, he wanted to be certain.

Bang! Bang! Bang!

He sent the steel-capped toe of his boot crashing into the first cell door that crossed his path.

'I fucking hate coming here,' he said.

They all did. These four men would rather be taking a serial killer to court than searching a woman's cell.

'Chances are you'd get in less trouble handling a bloke like Ivan Milat,' explained an officer from the Special Operations Group (SOP). 'It's very difficult for a male to go in to do a ramp in a woman's cell. They are always making complaints about us. They'll say we burst in on them when they were naked to have a bit of a look. Or they'll say we tried to touch them up or something. They're always making false allegations.'

So today the SOP were being particularly cautious; in this case by being outlandishly loud.

The men drove the soles of their shoes into the concrete with every step, the hard rubber tread slapping against cement. Sent to Mulawa on this day to execute a series of cell searches – looking for drugs, weapons and phones – the foursome were a 450kg tsunami of sound raging down the wing.

'It's not ideal because it certainly takes away the element of surprise,' the officer continued. 'It gives them time to hide whatever they have. But at the end of the day we would rather spend a little longer searching to find whatever it is than burst in on two girls having sex and cop a complaint.'

The officer slammed his fist into the door before announcing himself.

'This is a cell search,' he said. 'We're coming in. Male officer entering.'

He was sure he'd given her time to get ready . . .

'We walked in and she was in her lingerie,' the officer said. 'She was standing in the middle of the cell with her undies pulled up into a G-string and her boobs almost popping out of her bra.'

The officer went red.

'Oh,' he said. 'Would you like to get dressed?'

The inmate laughed. 'No ... but I can get *undressed* if you like?'

The woman licked her lips before slowing reaching around to her back. She unclasped the latch and her bra fell to the floor.

'Whoops,' she said. 'I better pick that up.'

She turned away from the officers and slowly bent over. She stuck her near-naked bum into the air. The woman stretched to the ground, legs straight, cheeks high, before sweeping the underwear from the floor and snapping to attention. And then she started to suck her thumb.

'She stood there asking us if we had anything else to suck on,' the officer said. 'It was fucking uncomfortable and a situation none of us wanted to be in. But we should have known better because this particular inmate had a reputation for this sort of thing. She was a real manipulative prisoner. She was one who would use her body to get what she wanted.'

Indeed, he should have known better. After all, men had murdered for the woman dubbed Belinda Van Evil.

Van Evil

Belinda Van Krevel stood by the window she had just opened and shivered.

It's fucking freezing, she thought. The curtains danced as the frigid August air poured through the opening, the light-weight cotton turning tutu.

Belinda took a deep breath before putting her face directly into the winter wind. Head now sticking out the window, she looked first left, then right.

The street was dark, quiet and empty.

Perfect.

She flicked her wrist and shut the window, but not all the way. Before leaving the room, the one facing out onto the working-class Albion Park street – brick veneer three-bedroom homes, not housing commission but close – she made sure the plastic latch on the 'slider' hadn't caught.

She walked into her room.

'Are you awake, sweetie?' she said to her two-year-old daughter, Tia, tucked snuggly in bed.

There was no response. Belinda pulled back the blanket and nestled down. She planted a kiss on the sleeping child, smiled and closed her eyes.

And then she waited . . .

Soon there were 'weird noises', as she would later report, 'like someone getting killed'.

In fact, the noises were not weird. They were horrific.

'Fucking die!' a man screamed as Belinda carefully cupped her hands around her child's ears. 'Die, you fuck!'

The murderous demands were coming from the very next room, muffled only by plaster and evenly spaced timber studs.

There was a thud followed by a yell – a different voice this time: *'Arrrggggh!'*

Next came a whacking noise. *Thwat!*

209

'I said fucking die,' the voice boomed, the wall doing little to muffle the murder.

Others noises followed – crashes, splats and whacks.

'Please don't,' cried Belinda's father, Jack. 'I beg you. Don't do it. I don't want to die.'

More whacks and grunts.

'You fucking paedophile bastard!' the attacker shouted. 'You'll never molest a kid again.'

Then all was quiet. The noises had stopped.

Belinda smiled.

'Go back to sleep, sweetie,' she said as her hands left her child's ears.

'What's happened to poppy?' Tia asked, awoken by the sounds next door.

Belinda pulled up the covers. 'Nothing. Must have been a nightmare.'

And what a nightmare it was. Jack Van Krevel, a 48-year-old Dutch immigrant and builder who had worked hard to raise his two children on his own after his wife left him, was hacked to death in his bed. In the early hours of August 2000, an intruder jumped through the open window of his Wollongong home and struck him 25 times with a tomahawk and a fire poker, before stabbing him 16 times with a knife.

His daughter, Belinda Van Krevel, did nothing about the weird noises, the ones that sounded like 'somebody getting killed'. Instead, she stayed in bed.

Still, even after her assurances, her child wouldn't sleep. *Is Poppy okay? Can you go and look?*

But Belinda wouldn't. The 19-year-old got up and put on a kids video in a bid to placate Tia.

'Go back to sleep,' she said. 'It's all okay.'

About an hour later, it wasn't.

'We have to get in the car,' Belinda said as she pulled her baby girl from the bed. 'We're going for a drive.'

She walked past her father's room, out of the house and hopped in her car. She arrived at Warilla Police Station 90 minutes after she'd first heard the 'weird' noises coming from Jack Van Krevel's room.

She told the police that she'd left her bedroom after hearing the noises and saw blood on the floor in the hall. She said she didn't know what had happened or if anyone had been hurt, but she decided to put her daughter in the car and drive the ten kilometres to the police station.

Keith Schreiber was arrested the next day. Schreiber was the best friend of Belinda's brother, Mark Valera, who himself was a double-murderer who had been sentenced to life imprisonment just two weeks before. Schreiber admitted to killing Jack Van Krevel for 'what he had done to Mark, Tia and Belinda'.

Van Krevel's brother was one of the most infamous men to ever come from Wollongong. An alleged Satanist, Valera had murdered former Wollongong Mayor Frank Arkell and shopkeeper David O'Hearn, becoming the youngest man ever to be sentenced to life without the possibility of parole when he was convicted of the two murders in 2000. He was just 21. Valera, 19 at the time of the killings, partially decapitated and disembowelled one of his victims. When confessing to police, he alleged he had been raped by his father, Jack Van Krevel, over a period of ten years. Valera also said he regularly spoke with his friend and fellow alleged Satanist Schreiber about killing him and how to dissect and dispose of the body.

Soon Schreiber was in custody too, exactly two weeks after a magistrate had handed down the record sentence to his best friend.

Police established that Schreiber had arrived at Van Krevel's house at around midnight on 18 August and entered through a window that had been left open. He didn't have a weapon but found a tomahawk axe propped up next to the garage door. Schreiber then walked into Van Krevel's room and attacked him with the axe while alleging the man was a paedophile.

'This is for them!' he screamed while hacking at him with the tomahawk. 'You bastard!'

The initial blows did not kill Van Krevel, so the attacker went and searched for another weapon. Schreiber returned with a fire poker and repeatedly smashed the man over the head until he was bludgeoned unconscious. He finished the murder by partially decapitating Van Krevel with a knife.

Schreiber told police he killed the man then went and opened Belinda's door to look in on her. He helped himself to a glass of water from the kitchen tap before leaving the scene of the horrendous murder through the very same window he had originally entered.

'Well, he won't be doing anything more to Tia,' he told police during a recorded statement.

Police asked him if he thought Belinda would be glad that he had killed her father.

'I hope so,' the confessed murderer said.

But the plot thickened . . .

'Were you having an affair with Belinda?' the police asked.

'Irrelevant,' Schreiber replied. But when pressed he admitted he was having a relationship with his best mate's sister. 'Sort of, yeah.'

In documents submitted during Schreiber's trial, Belinda's mother, Elizabeth Carroll, claimed her daughter had offered Schreiber $2000 to kill Jack Van Krevel. She said her daughter had been seduced in a car by Schreiber when the pair had 'bongs' shortly after Valera's trial.

Carroll told the court the pair had agreed for her ex-husband to be murdered and for Schreiber to 'hack him up into pieces and throw him into the Kiama blowhole'.

Schreiber later admitted to police that Belinda had spoken to him about killing her father. 'I didn't know if she was serious,' he said.

More details emerged . . .

Belinda was with Schreiber on 17 August, the day before the murder. The pair met at the Albion Park railway station before continuing to the Shell Harbour shopping centre. It was there that Schreiber bought black cotton gloves from Best & Less; the same gloves he would use to conceal fingerprints during the murder he would commit later that night.

The couple parted ways shortly after, and Belinda went home to watch *Home and Away* with a friend. The friend left and Belinda went to bed – after she made sure a window was open and an axe was propped up against the garage door . . .

In 2001, two years after the murder took place, Belinda Van Krevel, 22, pleaded guilty to soliciting the horrendous tomahawk murder of her father, which sent blood spattering all over the walls, floor and ceiling of her childhood home. Belinda admitted to telling Schreiber that her father had been interfering with a family member and that she wanted him dead.

During Van Krevel's trial, police alleged that hate and greed had motivated her to order her father's death. Belinda and her incarcerated brother, Mark, were the sole beneficiaries to her father's estate.

Belinda was originally charged with murder but pleaded guilty to the reduced charge of soliciting murder after a key witness for the prosecution 'fell through'.

She was found guilty and sentenced to six years in prison. She was paroled in 2007.

I Still Love Her, Even Though She Tried to Kill Me
Whack!

Belinda Van Krevel stabbed her partner, the latest love of her life, a 40-year-old who she lived with at Rockdale in Sydney's south-west.

Whack!

Again. This time harder. *Was she aiming at his heart?*

Whack! Whack! Whack! Whack!

The blows kept coming. The attack was frenzied and relentless.

'Stop it!' the man cried. 'It's me, Marshall. I'm not your father. Snap out of it!'

Bloodied and shaken, Marshall Gould subdued Belinda and dragged himself to the phone.

'Come and get me quick, Dad,' he said. 'She's gone crazy. She thinks I'm Jack and she's stabbed me.'

Gould left Belinda, now a sobbing mess, in the apartment and went to his father's house.

'You need to go to hospital, son,' said his father. 'She got you good.'

Gould checked himself into St George Hospital and was treated for multiple stab wounds to his body and a swollen right eye. Police were alerted and went to the hospital to take a statement from the injured man.

And this is where it gets bizarre. Belinda was already on a good-behaviour bond for assaulting and stalking Gould. But, still, he attempted to cover up his lover's latest crime by claiming he had been mugged by three men in a park. He gave a description of both the incident and his alleged attackers.

The police didn't buy it.

They issued a search warrant for his Watkin Street home, where they found both the blood and Belinda.

'She was charged that night,' said an officer. Van Krevel was sent back to jail after being convicted of one count of reckless wounding in relation to the stabbing. She was sentenced to a minimum of two years.

Marshall Gould stood outside the court on the day Belinda was handed her latest sentence, claiming he still loved her.

'I love her and I support her,' Gould said. 'She's had a troubled childhood.'

He also said he wasn't concerned it would happen again and would take her back when she finished her prison sentence.

The Boss

Prison officers who guarded Van Krevel during both her stints in Mulawa describe the notorious Wollongong woman as both a manipulator and a 'prison boss'.

'She would use her brother to try to intimidate all the other inmates,' said a current officer who asked not be named. 'She would say, "I'm Mark's sister," and he would get them if she asked him to. He was, of course, the "Butcher of Wollongong", and that association certainly intimidated a lot of the other girls.'

Belinda was also tough in her own right.

'She was very feared,' the officer continued. 'None of the other girls would mess with her. She was very dangerous, and the thing that made her dangerous was that she was willing to take a situation further than the other girls. You could see she had the propensity to be violent. She was a bit mad and the other girls knew it.

'She was the boss of a wing called Brady. No one would fuck with her because of who she was. She also had some high-profile friends inside. But while she was tough, I reckon most of the fear she instilled in others came from her crimes and that fact that she was the Butcher's sister.'

As a boss, Belinda never went without.

'You could tell she was a top dog because of what she had in her cell,' the officer said. 'She always had the best of everything. If there was something you could have in prison, she had it. And she very rarely had to use a buy-up – that is, to purchase anything herself. But she had everything. She was given things by other girls who tried to get on her good side. She had all the best clothes, the best shoes, the best of anything you could get in prison.'

Van Evil was never charged with an act of violence against a fellow inmate or officer during her combined eight years in prison.

'She didn't have to do the violence herself,' the officer explained. 'She got everyone else to do it for her. She had a little wing full of cronies who would do all her dirty work. They would go and assault people for her. Her crime was so violent that others feared her before she went in. She was very young, but she organised the whole lot. She was manipulative and very well known in the system.'

Van Krevel was also attractive, and she would use her looks to her advantage.

'She would use her looks and her good body to manipulate everyone,' the officer continued. 'She used to give the squads hell. During raids she would stand in front of her cell in nothing else but a bra and her undies. We were glad to see the back of her.'

The officer's remarks about Belinda being an extrovert are supported by her extraordinary behaviour during a parole board hearing in 2006. Arguing to be released after serving the six years for soliciting the murder of her father, Belinda put on a show for the parole board via a video link from Dillwynia Jail. While waiting for the full parole board to assemble, Van Krevel performed calisthenics, yoga and rhythmic gymnastics to the camera while speaking to those already in the court.

'I'm full of energy,' she said. 'I just can't sit.' Then she moaned while pushing herself against the back of a chair and sat on the table cross-legged.

Remorse and Regrets?

Belinda Van Krevel was released from prison in 2015 after serving her two-year sentence for stabbing Gould. She opened up about both her crimes in a tell-all interview with Channel 9's *60 Minutes*.

'I know what happened,' she told reporter Allison Langdon about her brother Mark's two murders. 'Why would a 19-year-old kid, boy, get up in front of the whole world and say that his father had raped him every day of his life if it's not true? So he can, what, make a fool of himself and embarrass himself? No 19-year-old boy's going to say that.

'He [Jack Van Krevel] drove him to do what he did. He's the one that should be in jail. Not my brother.'

Van Krevel went on to blame her father for the two killings committed by her brother, Mark Valera.

'Mark's innocent,' Belinda said. 'Mark's the innocent one. He was the victim, not David O'Hearn, not Frank Arkell, Mark.'

Belinda showed no remorse for soliciting the murder of her father, who she claimed was a sex offender.

'He deserved what he got,' Van Krevel said. 'As far as I was concerned, there was no other way out. I was just happy that Jack wasn't alive anymore. Without a doubt it was worth it.'

Kathy Yeo

Always in Love

'What is she doing?' the guard asked. 'Really? She has the nerve to come back here? To turn up and face all of us after everything that's happened?'

The officer snarled at the woman who had just entered the visits section at Emu Plains Correctional Centre. The woman walked over to sit down with one of Australia's most notorious female criminals – the 'psychotic nurse' who cut off her ex-boyfriend's head – Kathy Yeo.

'Oh no,' the officer said as the two women tongue-kissed. 'That's not on.' She shook her head as her former colleague put her hands between the inmate's legs.

It can be revealed for the first time that a female officer was sacked for having a sexual relationship with Kathy Yeo, the infamous man-murderer you are about to meet.

And, stunningly, the relationship continued after she lost her job.

'Her name was Riley,' said an inmate who asked to remain anonymous. 'She was having an affair with Kathy Yeo for some time before they found out. They were busted in the pottery room in about 2008. We all knew it was going on, so it wasn't a surprise. Kathy was very open about it.

'But what *was* a surprise was that they stayed together after she was sacked.'

Both guards and inmates were surprised when the former 'hard-nut' officer came back to the jail to visit Yeo.

'I couldn't believe it,' another inmate said. 'The officers would just stand in the visits and shake their heads in disgust. Here was this chick, one of the strictest screws, suddenly on the other side of the fence – not watching the crims or bossing them around – but sitting with them. One of them.'

While the officers couldn't believe it, they should have. Kathy Yeo was fatally attractive. The officer was just the latest in a long line of law-breaking lovers . . .

Heads Up

The nurse winked at her patient. 'How about it then?' she asked. 'You keen?'

The recovering heroin addict nodded. 'What do you think?'

It was a rhetorical question. Of course he was interested. Who wouldn't be? This was every red-blooded male's fantasy.

Christopher Dorrian, 32, was being propositioned by an attractive nurse – young, vivacious and utterly sexy.

This only happens in pornos, right?

No. It was happening to the university student who had recently got off the gear and vowed to fix his life.

'Let's go then,' the nurse replied. 'Follow me.'

The naughty nurse led Dorrian into an adjacent vacant room. She locked the door before ripping off her clothes. And then they had sex – hard, fast and passionate. They both climaxed quickly, the risk of being caught sending them into an erotic fit.

More storeroom sex was to follow. Kathy Yeo, 26, would fuck Dorrian every time he turned up for an appointment.

'I haven't done a thing wrong,' Yeo told her nursing supervisor when she was questioned about her behaviour. 'I don't know what you're talking about.'

Yeo was fronted by the Assistant Director of Nursing shortly after she began her clinical copulation. Rumours were rife that she was using the psych unit to lure lovers to bed. There were suggestions that she was sleeping with several patients. Fellow staff, too.

Yeo denied the claims and was spared the axe. Dorrian wasn't so lucky . . .

Police pulled the suspicious-looking sports bag from the river. The bag stank, was an ominous size and was covered in blood.

This isn't good.

The officer unzipped the bag.

Oh fuck!

He immediately gagged. He attempted to speak to his colleagues, but his muffled cries were unintelligible thanks to the dry-retching. Instead, he pointed at the open bag.

Some officers spewed.

Christopher Mark Dorrian's head was found in a sports bag that had washed up on the shore of the Cooks River in Sydney's inner-west on 21 June 1997. Police had little problem establishing the identity of the victim, given that Dorrian's identification had been left in the bag. They weren't so lucky with the rest of his body – it was never found.

Police soon turned their attentions to a psychiatric nurse named Keng Hwee Yeo. Investigators learned the nurse had been in a relationship with the man who had been decapitated. Keng Hwee, who called herself 'Kathy', had recently left her long-term partner after falling in love with Dorrian, who was a patient at her clinic. The pair began their affair in the clinic before moving in together after Yeo ended her relationship with 41-year-old Raymond Galea.

Dorrian and Yeo were happy at first, but the relationship soon deteriorated. Dorrian began to have his doubts about the nurse and told her he was considering 'moving on'. Yeo became distraught and did all she could to keep her man. It has been alleged she even attempted to 'get him using' heroin again so she could assert her control. But Dorrian was done. He told Yeo that it was over and asked her to leave his house.

Yeo went straight back to Galea, who welcomed her back with open arms. But while she resumed having sex with her former lover, she was still in love with her former patient. Yeo is alleged to have stalked and harassed Dorrian. After he repeatedly rebuffed her pleas to take her back, Yeo borrowed a gun from Galea and shot the man twice in the face.

Yeo then called on Galea.

'I need help,' she said. 'I've killed him. What do I do now?'

Galea knew. 'We need to get rid of the body.'

Easy Time

Yeo was sentenced to 24 years in prison for murdering and decapitating Christopher Dorrian. Galea, the love-struck punching bag, was convicted as an accessory after the fact and sent to jail for eight years. Galea went to the victim's house following the murder and helped Yeo cut up Dorrian's corpse. Only his head has ever been found.

Justice Michael Grove, the sentencing judge, said the killing was a 'horrific murder that was well planned and clearly not the result of sudden passion or impulse'.

Yeo appealed the sentence. Here is the court's ruling.

YEO, Keng Hwee (Kathy) – CCA, 23.2.2005
Sheller JA, Sperling & Adams JJ
Citation: R v Yeo [2005] NSWCCA 49
Conviction and sentence appeals.
Murder.
24-year sentence with no possibility of parole for 18 years.
Appellant was jointly tried with Raymond Galea, who was charged with being an accessory after the fact to murder.

At the outset of the trial, each of the accused sought a separate trial. These applications were refused. Both appellant & Galea had previously been tried on a charge of murder &, in the alternative, of being accessories after the fact. Appellant was convicted of murder but Galea was acquitted of murder & convicted of being an accessory after the fact. Both those convictions were quashed by the CCA & new trials ordered. Galea could not be retried on the murder charge. Appellant did not give evidence at either trial.

Galea did not participate in the commission of the murder. His culpability arose from his knowledge that the appellant had committed the murder &, with that knowledge, acted with the intention of assisting her to escape detection or prosecution. The appellant & Galea had been in a de facto relationship. Appellant left Galea & entered into a sexual relationship with the deceased while working as a nurse in a psychiatric hospital. The deceased was a patient in that hospital. Appellant obtained a pistol from Galea & subsequently shot the deceased in the head, killing him. She told Galea about the killing & both she & Galea dismembered the body for disposal.

Joint trials – whether separation wrongly refused – nature of prejudice – retrial following quashing on appeal – whether Crown significantly changed case – whether bound by way 1st trial was conducted – whether abuse of process – significance of bail conditions – whether double punishment.

Conviction & sentence appeals dismissed.

Yeo was sent to Mulawa, and she was welcomed with open arms.

'All the girls liked her as soon as she came in,' said a former Mulawa officer. 'She was a bit of a celebrity, and they were immediately drawn to her. She never got stood over or anything like that, and I think a lot of the heavies in there respected her because her crime was against a man. It would have been different if she was a baby killer. But, to be honest, she was a bit of a nothing inmate. She didn't cause trouble and kept a pretty low profile once she was in.'

Women who served time with Yeo have nothing but good things to say about the woman who threw her former boyfriend's head in the creek.

'She got on with everyone,' said an inmate who asked to remain anonymous.

'She was sweet and we all liked her.'

Victoria Schembri shared a house with Yeo during her incarceration for fraud.

'She was inspirational, intelligent and one of my best friends,' Schembri said. 'She was a motivator and someone who inspired you to better yourself. She encouraged me to enter the prison debating group and taught me how to use words to inspire others. She was so lovely to me and taught me a lot.'

Schembri admitted to knowing nothing about Yeo's past until she enquired.

'What did I know about her?' Schembri said. 'Nothing at first. But others told me she had killed her partner. I found out that she chopped him up. They found one part of his body and never the rest.'

Inmates and officers alike often questioned Yeo about the whereabouts of her former lover's body. It has become one of Australian crime's million-dollar questions.

'She will never, ever reveal what she did with the rest of him,' Schembri said. 'She always kept that very private and would tell everyone that she couldn't remember what she did.'

Yeo, the model inmate, has become religious since being sent to prison for murder.

'You would never pick her as a killer,' Schembri continued. 'She used to go to church every week. She went to all the Bible study classes, and she tried to help everyone in the jail.'

Yeo also became a teacher.

'She was constantly educating herself and tutoring other inmates,' Schembri said. 'As a person, you could not find someone better. She was not at all what you would expect.'

And, of course, she continued to keep a lover . . .

Other Deadly Dames
The Worst of the Rest

Australian prisons have housed some of the worst women in the world. You have already met the psychotic self-slasher who has been deemed 'too dangerous to be released'; the body-butchering cook dubbed Australia's very own Hannibal Lecter; the helicopter-hijacking sweetheart; the man-manipulating siren; and most recently the psychotic head-chopping nurse. But there are more – oh so many more. From Tilly Devine and the 'Razor Gangs' of the 1920s to Amirah Droudis – the woman who stabbed to death the former wife of Man Monis, the terrorist behind the Lindt Café siege, and set her body alight – places like Mulawa have seen them all. But the crimes these women committed on the outside is not always a reflection of who they will become once inside. You will never have heard of some of the women who have been singled out as prison matriarchs.

'There were always two main top dogs in the jail when I was there,' said a former prison officer who served at Mulawa for almost 15 years. 'They were Debbie Rogers and Mel O'Ryan. They were both absolutely crazy, violent and right at the top of the food chain. They had eyes that would cut straight through you. They hated officers with a passion, and they were the ones who set all the rules for the girls back in the 90s. They set the prison code, and they also enforced it. For me, the toughest was Mel O'Ryan. She was a drug addict and a real mean bitch. She thought nothing about bashing anyone and would often beat up young new girls for sex. She was in for drug-related crimes, and also for soliciting sex. And she was one mean woman, someone who certainly became a bit of a Mulawa legend.'

One inmate who lived under the reign of the woman called Mel'O said the prison enforcer was only violent when it came to drugs.

'I lived with Mel'O in both the 1980s and the 1990s,' she said. 'And, yeah, she was tough. But mostly she liked her drugs. If anyone had drugs and couldn't stand up for themselves, these girls would get them. It was all about drugs. I saw Mel'O give a girl a good hiding for no apparent reason. She flogged her, and I couldn't work it out because she was supposed to be her girlfriend – but I didn't ask any questions. I never had a problem with her, but I did see her stand over girls. I think she got her reputation because she would take on the screws. I reckon they were scared of her more than anything. Mel'O would get this big vein on her forehead, a big pulse, and she would just click out. She used to mix all her pills up and go crazy.'

The prison veteran also served time with Deborah Rogers.

'Debbie wasn't bad until they made her bad,' said the former inmate. 'Corrective Services did it to her. Debbie was all right at the beginning, but the medical staff sent her nuts. She was a softie at heart. She was involved in stabbing a girl in the 80s, but they drove her to it. She got no care for her disorders, and eventually she snapped. I lived with her when she came out of segro after four years. I lived with her in Conlon [wing]. Her problem was that she liked her drugs and would do anything to get them. If young girls had them, then she would take them. I never had drugs so I didn't have that problem. But, yes, other girls were intimidated by her – and they had reason to be.'

The veteran inmate, who has served time in jails in Queensland, Victoria and New South Wales, said the worst women she ever met were at Mulawa.

'I only served three years in Mulawa, but they were the worst of them all,' she said. 'I've been in and out for forty years and served time everywhere, but nothing compared to that place. There were assaults every day, drugs, rape . . . everything. I did a stint there in the early 90s and also one in the 2000s. Oh my God, I couldn't believe how violent it had become. The girls coming in off the streets were nuts because the drug scene had changed so much. In just a decade the man-made drugs had turned them into animals. The girls off the street were violent. I did three and a half in maximum security, and I had had one conflict. When I went back in 2002 I had conflicts and assaults every day. I used to buy the *Sunday Telegraph* every week and put it down the front and back of me in the non-working yard, because I was worried about being stabbed.

'They thought I had drugs, and they were willing to stab me. I didn't buy the paper to read it, but it saved my life. I knew it was going to happen, because I had been in jail for a long time. You learn all about body language. You know how to lip read. And you also get pretty good at hearing things.'

A current officer anointed the cousin of infamous male lifer Bassam Hamzy as Mulawa's present-day boss.

'Hamzy's cousin tried to get a gang going in Berrima Jail before it closed,' he said. 'But they just shipped her off and split them up. There aren't gangs as such in female jails; there are just cliques. And Hamzy ran a clique big enough to try and form a gang.'

The worst of the worst are kept in a place called the 'Female Supermax'. Officially, it is called the High Dependency Unit. It is a shocking section located in Sydney's Mulawa jail for women.

High-profile prisoner Harriet Wran, the daughter of former NSW Premier Neville Wran, was one of the unit's more recognisable guests.

'Harriett got placed there on full protection straight-away,' a current and high-ranking officer said. 'That was just because she was very high profile, vulnerable and weak. She would have got stood over from the beginning. The depart-ment forced her into that protection, knowing what would have happened to her. She was shacked up with a former prison officer called Sharon.

'Sharon tried to kill her husband last year, and he was an officer. They are both in one-out cells at the High Depend-ency Unit. It is very similar to the Goulburn HRMU [the infamous men's Supermax]. And life in there is just horrible. They are segregated. They have a little yard out the back, little kitchens, very high security. There are 12 cells and an identical number of officers to inmates. It's one for one.

'It is the worst by far. All your heavies are there, all your high-profiles. It's our only maximum-security facility for women anywhere. Parts of it are very old, but other parts are new. It's nothing like the men's jails, in terms of being intimidating. It's an old, run-down place in parts, but it's not scary. Once you're inside, it's not much like a jail at all. Most of the doors are just made of wood, aside from the big metal ones reserved for special guests.'

7

SHE-MEN

Sonya, Just Like Madonna

They approached the cell door with trepidation.

'You knock,' one of the two female inmates said. 'I don't want "It" getting pissed at me.'

The other woman shook her head. 'Fuck that – you're going in first.'

There was no way around it; the young inmate was going to have to knock. Moments before, a screw had ordered her to go and find It.

Summon It from Its lair.

And the only thing worse than what lay on the other side of the two-inch-thick reinforced steel door was the officer who issued the demand and his rock-hard baton.

The young inmate looked at the heavy door.

'There was a name written on the door,' she recalled. 'Not a first and last name, like every other cell door in the jail . . . Just a first name.'

Yep. Sonya. One name, like Madonna.

Knock! Knock!

Quiet at first, knuckles gently tapping steel. She didn't want a response.

'It's not going to hear that,' said the other girl, brave now that she was standing behind the designated knocker. 'Come on.'

Knock! Knock! Knock!

Harder this time.

'We'll be here all day,' said the braver-by-the-minute bystander. 'I think I can hear water. I think it's in the shower. Come on, let's get this over with.'

Yeah, fuck 'It'.

KNOCK! KNOCK! KNOCK!

The young inmate turned after beating the door, her knuckles red. 'Happy?' she asked.

The other woman nodded.

Still, there was no answer. Nothing.

'Oh well,' said the bystander. 'Let's go.'

Click!

The door latch gave way as the young inmate pushed instead of knocked. The door was open.

Oh shit. Is It here?

It was.

'We were confronted with something I can never forget,' recalled the woman who had pushed the door open. 'It was in the shower. It was completely naked, and It was fucking another girl. It has this huge dick ... all hard and erect, pumping away. I wanted to throw up.'

Wait a minute ... *Dick? Hard? Erect?*

'Oh yeah,' she continued. 'It was a bloke called Sonya. A transgender inmate who used to be called Barry or something like that. We all thought she had been castrated, but no ... It had a dick and it worked just fine. Sonya was fucking a girl in the shower.'

Yep. Welcome to the NSW Department of Corrective Services – the only place in New South Wales where a man can simply claim he's a woman and be locked up in a female jail ...

Sonya is one of a select few who have served time in both men's and women's jails in Australia. Sentenced as a sex-offending truck driver, *he* became a maximum-security make-up wearing *she* in Mulawa Correctional Centre.

'I believe he was a truck driver who was in for rape,' said Victoria Schembri. 'From what I understand, he used to pick up hitchhikers and assault them while his girlfriend watched. Anyway, he first went to a men's jail, and then he came to Mulawa when he decided he was a woman.'

The truck driver began dressing like a woman while locked up. He grew his hair long, shaved his legs and told prison officers that he had changed his name.

'Yeah, he called himself Sonya,' Schembri said. 'He didn't have a last name. He would introduce himself as, "Sonya; one name like Madonna".'

Sonya was moved to Mulawa to serve the rest of his sentence as a woman.

'We were pretty surprised when he rocked up,' Schembri said. 'He was moved in with little fuss, and we were like, *What is that and what is it doing here?* We were pretty freaked out.'

Sonya looked, smelled and acted like a man – at least when he wasn't being watched by the guards.

'There was no denying he was a bloke,' Schembri said. 'He was a big, ugly bloke.'

Sonya looked nothing like a woman, according to Schembri. He/she may have worn eye shadow, but his masculinity was unmistakable.

'He was disgusting,' Schembri said. 'There was nothing feminine about him. You know when you see a woman who has trained at the gym and has been using steroids? Big calf muscles? Huge biceps? That really big, lean muscle? That was him.

'Yes, he was one big, ugly ranga,' Schembri continued. 'He had this thick, curly red hair. He sounded like a man. And he acted like a man. I mean, he would put it on when the guards were around. He wore the make-up, the nail polish. But it was all for show. It was for the officers.'

Sonya kept to himself at first. The women he was locked up with assumed he had been castrated and was not a sexual threat. They also assumed he was interested in men – not women. But then Sonya began telling stories.

'He did pottery class with us, and he would brag about how he'd owned a brothel before he came in,' Schembri said. 'He told us that he used to sleep with all the prostitutes to test them out. He said they would tell him he was the best root they'd ever had. He said he was an expert lover. It was the first indication we had that he was into women. Looking back, I think it was all part of a ploy to get us interested in him.'

Soon the rumours started. Women started claiming that he had a penis. Not just a penis . . . a fully functional penis that he was attempting to use.

'An Asian woman came up to me and told me she had seen Sonya's dick,' Schembri said. 'Until that point, I thought he may have had it cut off or something. But this woman came up and told me that Sonya had pulled it out and shown it to her.'

Sonya allegedly began having sexual relations soon after revealing his penis.

'He started rooting the Asians,' Schembri said. 'I think he did it because the Asians were easy. They would do anything for a dick in jail. They were always the ones who were caught with officers, always the ones who were caught with dildos in their cells. He kept it quiet, but they all started speaking about it. Word got around.'

Still, no one was sure. Did he really have a dick? And, if so, did it work? Surely he was taking some type of medication?

'He started sexually harassing everyone,' Schembri said. 'It was only verbal but it was crude. He started making as all feel really uncomfortable. You never wanted to be alone with him, that's for sure.'

And soon the rumours were confirmed . . .

*

'Hey, where's that chocolate?' Sonya said. 'I have an idea.'

Sonya's room was heaving. Most of the girls from the wing had come to his cell to help celebrate his birthday. Sure, not many of them *liked* Sonya, but he had smuggled in a cache of drugs for the occasion. He had chocolate, too.

The girls, flying high and partying hard, paid him little attention as he turned and placed the block of Cadbury in a bowl before putting it in the microwave. But they did notice him taking off his clothes.

'Ever licked chocolate off a dick?' he asked.

The girls shrugged. Whatever. It was a party.

'I'll give it a crack,' said one of the women. 'Come on. Dip that stick.'

Sonya took the bowl from the microwave. Stark naked, he spread himself on the floor before pouring the melted chocolate on his stomach and then his genitals.

The obliging woman went to work, her tongue darting across his body, collecting the warm treat.

'What the fuck!' shouted one of the girls, pointing down at his penis. 'Look at that.'

'He has a fucking stiffy!' yelled another girl. 'A full-on erection.'

The party suddenly stopped.

'That's when the penny dropped,' said Schembri. 'When we knew he was just a man pretending to be a women. Sonya had a birthday party in 2008. She had all the girls in there and they were doing drugs and whatever. Anyway, she got a hard-on in front of everyone. "She" was supposed to have been castrated. That's what we thought, anyway. She got this chocolate and they poured it over his cock. It was like a bucks or something. And then he got a hard-on. Everyone was a bit wary of him until then, but after that he was seen as a genuine threat.'

Sonya soon became brazen.

'He started hitting on everyone,' Schembri said. 'Absolutely everyone. He would try and stand over every pretty girl in the jail and convince them to be his girlfriend. Everyone was terrified of him.'

The guards did little to stop him.

'He was always kept one-out,' Schembri said. 'He wasn't allowed to share a cell with anyone. But that's pretty much the only thing stopping him. The guards were a little bit timid with him. They didn't want to be seen as persecuting him, because it was a touchy subject.'

Sonya was not stupid. He knew that he was only one slip-up away from being returned to a men's jail. And, oh boy . . . Imagine what the men would do to him, knowing he had been locked up as a woman?

'He was a sicko,' Schembri said. 'A sex offender who pretended to be a woman so he could prey on women in a women's jail. But he was also careful. He would never rape a girl or anything like that. He could have. He was big and strong enough. But the threat of being returned to a men's jail stopped him from doing it.

'Sonya knew that he would be out of there if he ever got in trouble, so he didn't get into fights either. But he was cunning. He had another girl do all his dirty work. He used to get this girl, a very tough Aboriginal girl, to do his bashings. She was a fighter and would do anything for money.'

And soon he had a girlfriend.

'He ended up with a girl called Martina,' Schembri said. 'Everyone knocked him back except her. She denied they were having sex, but we knew they were.'

And they knew without a doubt when they were sent to collect Sonya from his cell.

'We were told to go and find him,' Schembri said. 'We knocked on the door because an officer was looking for him. There was no answer, but we could hear the shower. So we pushed it open, and there he was with his girlfriend, fucking her in the shower. He was never supposed to be in his room with anyone alone. They were busted heaps of times after that.'

So how did Sonya end up in Mulawa? Well, all he had to do was claim he was a woman. Yep, that's right. Any man can rock up to reception and say, 'Nah, mate. I'm not going to Goulburn or Long Bay. I'm a chick. Sure, I have hairy arms, an Adam's apple and, well, a penis, but, seriously, I'm a woman. I changed my name from Barry to Beatrice yesterday.'

And with that, at least in New South Wales, the inmate will be sent to a women's jail. This is the controversial policy that allows the likes of 'Sonya, one word like Madonna', to choose between being locked up with women or men. First implemented in 1996 under the *Transgender (Anti-Discrimination and Other Acts Amendment) Act*, I found it so astonishing that I have included the NSW Department of Corrections policy in its entirety.

Management of Transgender and Intersex Inmates.
Corrective Services NSW.
7.23.2
POLICY

A recognised transgender person must be treated as a member of the sex recorded on their identification proof (e.g. birth certificate, birth registration) showing that they are a recognised transgender person.

Self-identification as a member of the opposite gender is the only criterion for identification as transgender. Transgender and intersex inmates are to be managed according to their identified gender.

This policy also acknowledges and provides guidance for persons that do not identify as either male or female.

A person received into custody must be managed as the gender with which they identify at the time of their incarceration, regardless of their identified gender in previous periods of incarceration.

An intersex person, or a person who self-identifies as transgender, has the right to be housed in a correctional facility of their gender of identification unless it is determined through case management that the person should more appropriately be placed in a correctional centre of their biological sex. The decision for this placement will be based on:

- the nature of their current offence and criminal history (for example, crimes of violence and/or sexual assault against women or children)

239

- *custodial history (for example, previous management problems which impacted on the safety of other persons or the security of the correctional centre)*
- *perceived risk(s) to the continuing safety of the transgender inmate and/or other inmates from the transgender inmate.*

Recognised transgender, transgender and intersex inmates will have the same classification and placement options as all other inmates.

Recognised transgender, transgender and intersex inmates will have the same access to services and programs as other inmates in the correctional centre where they are housed.

If, during their incarceration, an inmate makes an application to be identified and treated as a transgender person, the inmate is to be treated as a transgender person who has just been received into custody.

7.23.3 PROCEDURES

7.23.3.1 Addressing recognised transgender, transgender and intersex inmates

Recognised transgender inmates are to be addressed by name and according to their recognised sex.

Transgender and intersex inmates are to be addressed by their chosen name and according to their identified gender. Male-to-female transgender inmates are not to be called by their male given names (regardless of what is recorded on their warrant file) or referred to as 'he'; they are to be called by their female names and referred to as 'she'. A similar principle applies for female-to-male transgender inmates. Accordingly, all accommodation records are to be amended to reflect the inmate's identified gender.

An inmate who does not identify as either male or female is to be addressed by their chosen name and clarification sought from the inmate as how they are to be addressed.

7.23.3.2 Escorting recognised transgender, transgender and intersex inmates

A recognised transgender person must be treated as a member of the sex recorded on their identification proof (e.g. birth certificate, birth registration) and will be escorted as such.

Until transgender inmates, intersex inmates and inmates that do not identify as either male or female, have completed the induction and screening process and have been assigned to a correctional centre, they are to be kept separated from all other inmates during escorts. This separation is to ensure the safety of all inmates and avoid the risk of physical or sexual assault incidents occurring during transit of:

- recognised transgender, transgender and intersex inmates from other inmates
- other inmates from recognised transgender, transgender and intersex inmates.

When the induction, screening and assessment has been completed and the inmate's placement decided:

- male-to-female and female-to-male transgender inmates assigned to a female correctional centre may be escorted with other female inmates, if the General Manager determines that there are no known safety or security concerns

- *male-to-female and female-to-male transgender inmates assigned to a male correctional centre are to be kept separate from all other inmates during escorts to avoid the risk of physical or sexual assault by other inmates in transit*
- *an inmate who does not identify as either male or female are to have escort conditions determined according to the assessment finding/s and placement in either a male or female centre.*

A recognised transgender inmate received into custody who has identification proof showing that they are a recognised transgender person, is to be sent to a correctional facility of their recognised sex.

All recognised transgender inmates received into custody who do not have identification proof showing that they are a recognised transgender person and who have a previous arrest/custody record as a different sex, must be sent to the Metropolitan Remand and Reception Centre (MRRC) for assessment and determination of placement.

Inmates that do not identify as male or female, who are received into custody must be sent to the MRRC for assessment and determination of placement.

7.23.3.4 Assessment for placement
When assessing a male-to-female transgender inmate, intersex inmate or an inmate that does not identify as either male or female for placement in a female correctional centre, the Case Management Team (CMT) from Silverwater Women's Correctional Centre must take part in the CMT assessment process at the MRRC.

Inmates identified as or suspected of having cognitive impairment and who identify as transgender, intersex or neither male nor female, must have their capacity for decision-making assessed in considering placement and medical intervention. Access to appropriate support services e.g. Additional Support Units should be considered in any placement decisions.

7.23.3.5 Searching and urinalysis

Except in cases of emergency, the strip and pat searching of a recognised transgender inmate is to be conducted by an officer of the same sex as the recognised sex of the inmate. However, where an officer is not comfortable with this directive, another officer (of the same sex as the recognised transgender inmate) should be assigned the task.

Transgender and intersex inmates must be asked their preference regarding the gender of the officer conducting strip and pat search procedures. Except in cases of emergency, the strip and pat searching of a transgender or intersex inmate is to be conducted by an officer of the preferred gender. The Officer in Charge is to assign an officer of the preferred gender to conduct the search procedure. However, where an officer is not comfortable with this directive, another officer (of the preferred gender) should be assigned the task.

If the transgender or intersex inmate expresses no preference, search procedures should be conducted by an officer of the gender of identification of the inmate.

Except in cases of emergency, an inmate that identifies as neither male nor female is to be asked their preference regarding *the gender of the officer conducting strip and pat search proce-dures. The Officer in Charge will then assign an officer of the preferred gender to carry out the procedure. However, where an officer is not comfortable with this directive, another officer (of the preferred gender) should be assigned the task.*

If the inmate that identifies as neither male nor female expresses no preference, search procedures should be con-ducted by a:

- *male officer if the inmate is placed in a centre or area of a centre that is designated to house male inmates*
- *female officer if the inmate is placed in a centre or area of a centre that is designated to house female inmates.*

Two officers should be present to supervise the urinalysis collection procedure. Where possible, both of these officers (or at least one of these officers) must meet the same sex/ gender requirements as those detailed above for searching.

7.23.3.6 Clothing and buy-up
The inmate clothing policy in OPM section 9 Inmate Private Property applies to recognised transgender, transgender and intersex inmates.

Recognised transgender inmates have the right to dress at all times in clothing appropriate to their recognised sex.

Transgender and intersex inmates have the right to dress at all times in clothing appropriate to their gender of iden-tification – including those inmates housed in correctional centres of their biological sex. Issue clothing and underwear appropriate to their identified gender is to be provided to transgender and intersex inmates.

Transgender and intersex inmates housed in correctional centres of their biological sex are to be able to purchase the same personal care items, cosmetics, clothing and underwear through the buy-up system as other inmates of their identified gender.

An inmate that does not identify as either male or female is to be provided with their preference in relation to clothing to be issued and purchase of personal care items, cosmetics, clothing and underwear through the buy-up system.

7.23.3.7 Access to medication and health services
For recognised transgender and transgender inmates who have not been prescribed hormone therapy in the community prior to custody, a case plan must be developed collaboratively by a multi-disciplinary team of Justice Health & Forensic Mental Health Network (JH&FMHN) staff, Corrective Services NSW (CSNSW) psychologists and an Offender Services & Programs (OS&P) staff member authorised by the Manager, Offender Services & Programs. Ongoing psychological interventions (as determined by the psychologist) are to be integral to the plan.

For recognised transgender and transgender inmates who have been prescribed hormone therapy in the community prior to custody, the hormone therapy must be continued and appropriately managed whilst in custody by the Health Centre General Practitioner in consultation with relevant JH&FMHN Clinical Directors. The inmate's case plan must be jointly developed by CSNSW and JH&FMHN staff. The plan should provide clear management guidelines including ongoing risk assessments for the inmate and others within the centre as well as determining appropriate psychosocial support.

Transgender inmates may make an application to have elective gender surgery, hormone therapy or other therapies of choice, specific to their needs at their own expense.

JH&FMHN personnel will undertake monitoring of recognised transgender and transgender inmates prescribed hormone therapy to determine the safety and efficacy of the treatment.

When an intersex inmate requires medication, they will be assessed and managed by JH&FMHN and CSNSW staff on an individual needs basis.

7.23.3.8 Rehabilitation and integration
Recognised transgender, transgender and intersex inmates are to be provided with the same access to services and programs as other inmates. Additionally, recognised transgender, transgender and intersex inmates are to have access to services specific to their needs such as peak community services and groups e.g. the Gender Centre and legal services which specialise in the area of transgender and intersex people.

7.23.3.9 Access to information
On reception, recognised transgender, transgender and intersex inmates are to be given a copy of annexure 7.19 Fact Sheet: Transgender and Intersex Persons in Custody.

Recognised transgender, transgender and intersex inmates may purchase or receive, through visits or by mail, publications that address the needs of recognised trans-gender, transgender and intersex people e.g. a magazine published by the Gender Centre.

Maddison Hall

Sonya was not the first man to terrorise the women of Mulawa. A transsexual killer called Maddison Hall went on an eight-month rampage, attacking up to ten women while locked up at the Sydney women's jail between 1999 and 2000. This is the incredible story of the sex-change killer who went from 'sucking men off' in Long Bay to allegedly getting a female prisoner pregnant in Mulawa.

Noel Crompton Hall decided he was a woman shortly after being convicted of murdering a hitchhiker near Mildura in 1987. Locked up in Long Bay Jail, one of New South Wales' most notorious male prisons, he began asking people to call him Maddison.

'He changed his name to Maddison Hall,' recalled a former Long Bay officer. 'He said Noel no longer existed and that he was now Maddison, that he was a woman.'

Noel was a big man. Tall and dripping with muscle, he could stand up to most men in the often violent – and some-times murderous – prison.

'So, yeah, it was weird to see him when he started getting around in miniskirts,' said the former officer. 'He was always homosexual to my knowledge, but he started getting around dressed as a woman. The boys loved it because he would go around sucking them all off and do whatever they wanted when it came to sex. He would offer himself to anyone for drugs.'

Hall claimed he was a woman trapped in a man's body. And authorities would soon agree. Despite having a fully functional penis, the inmate now known as Maddison was transferred to Mulawa in 1999. But before we get into what happened there, let's revisit what he did 12 years before, when he was a tattooed 26-year-old drug dealer.

Lyn Saunders slammed the bonnet and walked away from his car. It was stuffed. He was on the side of a dirt road somewhere in south-west New South Wales. Christmas was just three days away; he needed to get home. The 28-year-old had promised his mum that he would be there to unwrap his share of presents sitting under the family Christmas tree.

Saunders had little money, so his car was going to have to stay exactly where it was. The only thing that was moving was his thumb. He hoisted it high into the air every time the roar of a car engine sounded, momentarily overpowering the relentless, and highly annoying, chirping of crickets.

Vroooooooom!

The third car blasted past, sending wind, dirt and petrol fumes into his face. This was hopeless. Maybe he would have to walk to Adelaide?

Screecchaaa!

Finally. The sound of straining brakes snapped him from despair, and he looked down at the rubber skid marks the car had laid down on the road.

'Where you heading, mate?' asked the driver, passenger window already down.

'Adelaide,' Saunders replied.

'Jump in,' said the stranger. 'I'll take you as far as I can.'

Saunders was hoping he would be taken all the way to his family home in Adelaide, but he was okay with being dropped anywhere in South Australia. At worst, he was preparing to be dumped somewhere in Victoria. He never once for a moment thought he would be stuck in New South Wales. Forever . . .

The man walking his horses suddenly stopped. The animals continued along, walking from the road and onto the dirt, but the shock of what he was seeing brought the trainer to a standstill.

He had stumbled across the body of Lyn Saunders – what was left off him anyway.

The hitchhiker was stone-cold dead, his head ripped apart by a shotgun shell. The stranger who'd picked him up, Noel Crompton Hall, had fired the kill-shot point-blank into Saunders' face. Hall's sawn-off had already blasted one into his back, but that didn't kill the young man, so Hall aimed a little higher and moved the gun a little closer. He placed the shortened barrel, much easier to conceal than the full-length shotgun, into Saunders' mouth and pulled the trigger.

The pair had been arguing just before hitting the Victorian border, so Hall stopped his car, pulled out his gun and blew Saunders' head off. It is understood that the disagreement was over a small quantity of marijuana.

Hall then went back to Campbelltown, New South Wales, to his wife and his life. He acted like nothing had happened. He thought he'd got away with it. But he hadn't.

Eighteen months after the cold-blooded murder, *Australia's Most Wanted*, a popular prime-time TV program, aired pictures of the murdered man. The show detailed when Lyn Saunders went missing, when he was found and how he was killed.

Hall might have forgotten about the young man he'd murdered, but Saunders' mother hadn't – nor had the horse trainer, who was still having nightmares about blood and blasted brains. And the police told them they would never forget either ... and they didn't. Hall was arrested shortly after the episode of *Australia's Most Wanted* was aired. An anonymous tip-off led police to his front door.

Hall was arrested, charged, convicted and sentenced to life in prison. No one could have ever predicted that he would serve part of that sentence as a woman.

I'm a Woman, Get Me Out of Here

Maddison Hall successfully pleaded to be moved to a women's jail in 1999. She was taken to Mulawa and placed in a one-out cell in the maximum-security section of the jail.

Former Mulawa inmate Kat Armstrong admits that Hall was a difficult prisoner from the get-go.

'She could be horrendous at times,' Armstrong said. 'No doubt about it. She had an attitude. She was a loudmouth and she was domineering. But in saying that, there were women in there who could be ten times worse than her.'

Armstrong alleges that Hall became a target for the officers because of her attitude.

'She gave them a lot of mouth,' Armstrong said. 'She would take on officers all the time. Say, if we were locked down early one day, it would be her yelling out that it was a breach of rights, and she would make a complaint. She was seen as a troublemaker. And for her, being locked down was an issue. She couldn't get her medicine for days at a time when we were locked down. She relied on that medication, and because of that she would be the first one on the buzzer to complain. She was very vocal about most things.'

But Armstrong denies that Hall ever raped or sexually assaulted a fellow inmate. Hall was controversially and publicly shanghaied back into the men's prison system in 2000 after several women came forward and claimed they had been raped by the convicted killer.

Hall was moved from Mulawa to the Junee Correctional Centre for men after she was charged with sexually assaulting her cellmate.

'That is bullshit,' Armstrong said. 'I didn't witness anything of the sort. I lived in her wing and that is bullshit. She did have relationships with other women, but it was always consensual. If they have come out later and said that she has raped them or whatever, it's not true to my knowledge. That's not my understanding of Maddison Hall or my personal experience when it comes to Maddison Hall. I disagree with those allegations.'

But others don't, including former NSW government opposition leader Peter Debnam. In an explosive sitting of the NSW parliament in 2006, Debnam not only confirmed Hall sexually assaulted fellow inmates, but that he had also impregnated one.

'Yes he/she attacked a number of women,' Debnam told parliament. 'Yes, one of them ended up pregnant.'

A former Mulawa inmate also alleges Hall was a sexual predator.

'Oh, he attacked plenty of women,' she said. 'He had a fully functioning penis, and he used it. He got a girl pregnant. We knew her. And they ended up releasing her to cover it up. It was a huge embarrassment for them, so they let the pregnant girl out.'

The Department of Corrective Services denied that Hall had impregnated a fellow inmate at Mulawa.

'We have nothing on our records to suggest that has occurred,' a spokesman said.

And according to Armstrong, prison officials coerced the inmate into making false claims about Hall in a successful bid to have her removed from the prison. Hall was never convicted of any offence that was alleged to have occurred during her nine-month incarceration at Mulawa.

'I think she was moved because the officers didn't like her,' Armstrong said. 'I think they got trumped-up statements from these women. They wanted her out of there. There is so much bias and judgment from officers, especially when it comes to homosexuality, let alone transgender people. So many of the officers have a completely redneck attitude. To them, you are either a women or a man – there is no in between. She also wasn't liked by any of them because of her mouth.'

The Hall controversy continued, even intensified once she was cleared of charges; the complaints were unsubstantiated.

Now a man again, at least according to authorities, Hall prostituted himself to male prisoners for drugs and other favours at Berrima Jail. Hall was also allegedly harassed by both inmates and officers.

'He was certainly given a bit of a verballing,' said an officer who asked to remain anonymous. 'We called him an "It" and a tranny and stuff like that. The other inmates teased him too, but I never saw anyone assault him. And no one had to rape him. He would suck off anyone if they wanted it. He would whore himself around. No one needed to rape him, and I don't think anyone did.'

In 2000, shortly after being moved back into a men's jail, Hall remarkably – and successfully – sued the Department of Corrective Services for 'psychological trauma'. He was awarded $25,000 in an out-of-court settlement. So, was Armstrong correct when she alleged officers manufactured the sexual assault claims to have the troublesome prisoner removed from the women's prison system? *Mmm.*

What is not in dispute is that the successful ruling made Hall a highly litigious man, and in 2001 he went to the Supreme Court in a bid to have his sentenced overturned under the 'Truth in Sentencing Act'. And once again he had a win. Hall's life sentence was repealed, cut to 22 years on top and 16 years and six months on the bottom.

With the prospect of being out in just five years, and 25 K in his pocket, Hall finally decided it was time to officially become a 'she'. With support from the Department of Community Services Gender Centre, Hall was given permission by Corrective Services to undergo full gender reassignment surgery.

A guard recalled taking Hall to the hospital for the procedure.

'She went in a man, and I took her home a woman,' said the officer. 'My partner on the job, who was a female, had to go into the surgery, which was weird, because they deemed [Hall] a woman, even though she was a man. She saw the operation. I wasn't allowed into the operation because I was a male. But I was in the ward when she came back, and I had to watch Hall with her legs spread, getting cleaned before the new dressing went on. Really, it was something I didn't have to see.'

Someone saw more. *Much more* . . .

Nip and Tuck

The boss approached a prison officer; the popular female staffer quietly going about her business.

'Hey, we have an inmate down in Wing 13, a protection prisoner, who needs a medical escort tomorrow,' the boss said. 'Would you like to do it?'

The young officer smiled, happy to be noticed.

The boss wants me for a job? Awesome. I must be doing something right.

'Sure,' she beamed. 'Of course.'

A smile crept across the boss's face too. In fact, he was straining to hold it back.

That's bizzare. He looks like he's about to start laughing.

'What?' asked the young officer. 'What's wrong?'

The boss started laughing. Hysterically.

'What?' she asked again. 'What are you laughing at?' The young officer finally caught on. 'Oh, it's like that, hey? So, who am I taking on the escort? This will be good.'

The boss stopped laughing, but only long enough to answer the simple question.

'Maddison Hall,' the boss blurted. 'And you are taking her for a sex-change operation.'

The young officer did not just take Maddison Hall to the surgery, but she watched on as the surgeon turned a man into a woman. The now former officer recalled every gory detail of the medical miracle.

And when I say gory . . . I mean GORY.

'I met [Hall] for the first time the morning after the boss asked me to do the escort,' the former officer said. 'It was a strange experience because I was pretty new to the job and had lived a sheltered life. I had never really even known a gay person, let alone a transsexual.'

The officer opened the cell, and the inmate was excited and ready to go. She was like a kid on Christmas Eve.

'She told me that she had been waiting for this day for ages,' the former officer continued. 'She was smiling and super happy. She told me she was paying for it herself. She said the department had stopped her from getting it done three times, so until now all she could do was have the hormone treatments. She spoke about her counselling and everything that she had done to prepare for it. She was so enthusiastic and happy that I couldn't help feeling happy for her. It was obviously something she was desperate to get done.'

The officer was greeted by the surgeon who would perform the gender-defying magic trick when she arrived at the hospital, inmate and fellow guards in her wake.

'We went into the surgery and the doctor asked us if we were okay with blood and gore,' the former officer recalled. 'He explained the procedure would be quite confronting before telling us what we would see.'

Yep. There one minute. Gone the next.

'I didn't have a problem with it,' the former officer said. 'It was my duty to be there to guard the prisoner, and I was going to do it. And aside from that, I was quite interested. It isn't every day that you get to see a man become a woman.'

The officers were briefed and the inmate was sedated. They were scrubbed down and dressed in surgical garb before being led into the operating theatre. Hall was waiting ... legs spread, what little she had hanging loose.

'The surgeon went over and sat on this low stool that was positioned between her legs,' the former officer said. 'And we were told to stand straight behind him. We had a bird's-eye view of the operation. We could see everything.'

Everything?

'Yep, we could see her penis,' the former officer continued. 'There wasn't much down there even before it was taken off because she had been on the hormones already. Her penis and testicles were tiny and shrunken. She was completely shaved down there too, and she looked like a baby with this tiny little penis and balls.'

Action. The show started.

'I thought there was going to be a lot of blood,' the former officer said. 'But there wasn't because he didn't cut her as such. It was all burnt off by way of cauterisation.'

The surgeon went for the penis first.

'There was this horrible burning smell when he started,' the former officer said. 'He began at the underside of the penis, cutting at the shaft. He went right round.'

Off it went, pulled away with a pair of medical tongs and placed in a silver tray.

'All that was left was a small bit of skin, which would later be used to make a clitoris,' the former officer explained.

Now for the balls.

'He then put an incision beside each testicle. After making the cuts, he stuck his fingers in the slits and just popped them both out.'

They didn't go into a silver tray. Each testicle was put into a separate jar.

'He then stitched the two incisions into one to make the labia,' the former officer continued. 'Then he put his thumb on the top of the wound and his finger on the bottom. He pulled the loose flesh up and he folded it into a vagina.'

And, just like that, Noel Crompton Hall was officially a woman. There could be no disputes this time.

'Well, it was all cosmetic,' the officer continued. 'It wasn't a functional vagina as such. The surgeon just did his best to make it look like one.'

'Where am I?' Maddison Hall asked the officer as she opened her eyes.

The officer smiled. 'You're in the recovery ward of a hospital. You've just had surgery.'

Maddison beamed, the grogginess suddenly gone.

'Nurse,' she shouted. 'Nurse!'

A woman dressed in white rushed to her side. 'Are you okay?'

Maddison was more than okay. She was a woman.

'I am fantastic,' she said. 'But I would be better if you could get me a mirror.'

Moments later, Hall had a mirror in her hand. She shoved it straight between her legs. 'Oh wow. That is just the most beautiful thing I have ever seen. It is gorgeous. I love it.'

The officer nodded.

'What could I say?' the former officer said. 'She was just so happy. I was posted by her bed, waiting for her to wake up. And when she came round and realised where she was and what had happened, she was just overjoyed. She called for the nurse straightaway and told her to bring a mirror. She was all bandaged up down there, but it was thin gauze, so you could see through it. She was pretty happy with the result.'

And the result was that she no longer had a penis.

'She was so happy to have it gone,' the former officer continued. 'She actually became very emotional. She told me that her penis repulsed her, and she felt sick every time she had to go to the toilet and look at it. She was even repulsed by having to wash. She said it was like it was someone else's.'

Man, I Feel Like a Woman

Noel Crompton Hall was now officially Maddison Hall and would soon be up for parole. She was already free from being a man, and she would soon be free from being in prison.

But Hall had already had one brush with 'soon'.

In 2006, she was about to be granted parole, but it was revoked at the eleventh hour. Her barrister, Philip Young, said the parole was revoked because of a media beat-up. He said it was the 'media blood sport of flushing out paroles'. To be fair, the media were relentless, but also, again to be fair, maybe with good cause.

'Sex-change killer will strike again' read the headline in Sydney's *Daily Telegraph*, nine days before the parole was revoked. Journalist David Fisher had obtained a letter from Hall's ex-wife, one that she had sent to the Attorney-General, expressing her concerns about the pending release.

'I believe Noel Crompton Hall is not of stable mind whatsoever and will repeat offend once back in society,' wrote the woman only identified by the paper as 'Sharon'.

'Noel and I have two children from our marriage. Along with believing Noel will very quickly reoffend once he is released, my biggest fear is he will try and locate his children, while both my son and daughter have expressed openly and strongly that they do not want any contact with him. Obviously I knew first hand the violent, twisted, lying nature of Noel Hall. I had been beaten by him and had ... the same gun [that he had used in the murder of Lyn Saunders] shoved in my face. It has taken me time, encouragement, family love, a new partner and a child to rise above it all, but honestly, the scars remain.'

The family of Lyn Saunders also took aim at the HIV-positive killer in the lead-up to his parole review. 'He is a clever individual and he has not done this [gender reassignment surgery] because he is a woman trapped in a man's body, but because he wants to screw with the system.'

No amount of hysteria could stop Hall from being released in 2010. After 22 years in jail, almost the maximum under the redetermined sentence, Hall was free.

Hall's story placed the issue of transgender firmly in the spotlight. The policy in New South Wales has been equally railed against and smiled upon.

'New South Wales provides strict direction at every step of the detention process around the appropriate manner in which trans-prisoners should be housed,' said Rebecca Leighton from the People for Sex Workers Rights group in Western Australia. 'And it does so wherever possible on the basis of their lived experience rather than the whims of prison authorities. It is not perfect, but it is clearly the most thought-out model currently existing in Australia.'

Armstrong, the former inmate turned advocacy worker, said a person has the right to choose whether he is a man or a woman.

'I think they should be allowed to go into their prison of choice,' Armstrong said, 'regardless of whether they have a penis or not. They are on such heavy drugs that the penis can't function anyway. They can't get an erection. So legally they are regarded as a female. That is why they don't need to have had the full sex-change operation. The support transgender people receive is minimal.'

But others disagree, including an inmate who knew Hall as both a man and then as a woman.

'What a joke,' he said. 'It's the greatest rort of all time. After that happened, we all sat back and wondered how we could do it too. Fuck, we would've all got around in miniskirts if it meant being shifted to a jail where you could shack up with a woman. Imagine how much fun you would have being locked up in a wing full of women.'

Cheryl and Wayne

Cheryl should have been happy. She wasn't. Sure, the dress still fit. That was a bonus. It had been five years since she had last worn it – the day she arrived at Long Bay Jail to begin her prison sentence. They had taken it off her and given her a green pair of trousers and baggy green shirt. She hated how the masculine garb made her look like a man. But as she walked out of the prison gate a free woman, a guard wishing her all the best out there in the real world, she decided that she no longer even liked the dress.

She preferred green.

Cheryl fumed as she walked the streets of Malabar, her face going from pink to bright red. She had just been released from jail after her longest ever stint, but there was no one waiting for her when she got out. There was no car to pick her up. No family member to give her a hug. No friend with an offer to go to the pub.

Wouldn't it be nice to get shit-faced?

Yep. There was no one. Cheryl was alone. It was just her and her pink dress.

Actually, it doesn't even fit. It's too loose.

Cheryl kicked a stone after deciding she hated the dress.

'Fuck this!' she screamed into the empty street, the morning gone and lunch not quite here. 'What am I going to do?'

Cheryl picked up the pace, charging to the boundaries of Malabar. Civilisation loomed. She suddenly had purpose. Soon, she was confronted by cars and chaos – she had hit the bustling Sydney suburb of Maroubra.

Cheryl started to sweat.

Cars. People. Open Space.

She looked across Anzac Parade and saw the golden arches of McDonald's. They called her name.

Yep. That's it. That's what I'll do.

Now full of intent, the light bulb that had gone off in her head was brightly burning, Cheryl played Russian roulette with the traffic. She didn't look, dodge or weave as she steamed onto the road.

And she didn't run.

Eyes firmly focused on the famous fast-food restaurant, she kept the same ploughing pace, as even as it was angry, forcing cars to swerve.

Geez, she must really need a Big Mac, the driver who almost collected her must have thought. *What the hell do they put into that special sauce?*

Having survived the highway – a minor miracle – Cheryl burst through the doors and thundered her way to the counter, not glancing at the menu for a moment.

Well, a girl knows what she wants.

'Hi, can I take your order please?' asked the McDonald's employee enthusiastically.

Cheryl replied by pressing the freshly broken bottle she had found on the street into the girl's neck.

'Yeah,' she shouted. 'You can take me order. Give me all your fucking cash, bitch. Give it to me or I'll jam this into ya throat.'

Ka-ching!

The register snapped open and the girl grabbed a fistful of notes. She slammed them on the counter.

Cheryl removed the bottle from the cashier's throat and grabbed the cash from the faux marble countertop.

'Thanks,' she said. And with that she turned and walked from the store. Yep. She didn't run. She walked. And, once outside, she stopped about five metres from the front door and sat down. And, hands above her head, cash in her lap, that's where she remained until she was picked up by the police.

'What took youse so long?' she asked as they snapped cuffs onto her wrists.

And soon she was back in green.

'She had finished her sentence and was released,' recalled a former officer who asked not to be named. 'As soon as she got out, she walked straight down the road to Maroubra and held up the McDonald's store. She just wanted to get caught so she could go back in. She literally went straight from the jail to the McDonald's store. And then straight back to jail.'

Why? Is jail food that good?

'No,' the officer laughed. 'She was in love. She had a partner in jail. A man called Wayne. And she wanted to get back to him. They shared a cell and were just like husband and wife. She couldn't be without him, so she did the hold-up just so she could go back to him.'

Hold on a minute . . . Husband and wife? Shared a cell?

'Oh, Cheryl wasn't quite what you would call a woman,' the officer continued.

'She was a man.'

Yep. Cheryl dressed like a woman. She walked like a woman. She spoke like a woman. But she had a penis and was locked up in Long Bay Correctional Centre – a male-only jail with a fearsome reputation.

'She was, in fact, one of the first transvestites we had in the system,' the former officer continued. 'And she liked it so much she never wanted to leave.'

This is a book about female prisons . . . but what the hell. Her name is Cheryl and she arrived in a dress.

Cheryl Gyson turned heads when she first arrived at Long Bay Jail wearing a dress.

'She was one of the first trannies we had in custody,' said the former officer who worked at Long Bay when Gyson was taken into custody. 'It was the early 90s and we had never seen anything like that before.'

A transvestite? What the . . .? The boys are going to have some fun with her . . .

'Seriously, we didn't know what to do with her,' the former officer continued. 'We were concerned she might be raped or bashed, even killed. Some of the hardest criminals in Australia were in Long Bay. It was a very rough jail back then. In fact, it still is.

'Being gay could get you killed. And here we had someone who was not only gay, but who also claimed to be a woman. So, given the situation, we thought the only thing to do was put her in protective custody – but even that wasn't going to ensure her safety.'

Cheryl was sent to Long Bay after being convicted of drug-related crimes.

'Oh, she was a junkie,' the former officer said. 'One look at her would tell you that. She was really skinny and really, really ugly. The drugs had taken their toll. She was immediately prescribed huge doses of methadone, and she admitted to being a horrendous addict.'

Did the officer mention ugly?

'That was an understatement,' the former officer continued. 'We would later get some trannies in there who were quite attractive. Nice faces, good bone structure and fake tits, but Cheryl, well, she was just plain ugly. A starved man who thought he was a woman.'

The reception process was almost complete. *Medical?* Check. *Classification?* Check. *Clothes?*

'What the fuck are they,' Cheryl demanded as she was handed a green pair of trousers and a matching shirt. 'They're men's clothes. Do I look like a man? I am all woman, if you haven't damn well noticed.'

The officer laughed. And then he walked off.

'She was given men's clothes to wear like everyone else,' said the former Long Bay officer. 'She wasn't happy, but she made do. She took her clothes back to her cell and she customised them to suit her. Back then they were given trousers, like a pair of long grey stubbies they wear at school, but green. She made sure she could get the smallest size possible so they were tight; they were ridiculously skinny. And then she rolled them up so they were three-quarters. She also made singlets from the shirts. That was her little way of showing everyone she was a girl. She wore everything different to the guys.'

Cheryl also demanded two towels whenever she took a shower.

'She would come out of the shower with one towel wrapped around her head like a lady with long hair,' the officer said. 'And she would wrap the other one around her chest so no one could see her tits, even though she had no boobs. We had another one in there soon after who did the same thing, but she'd gotten a boob job, so she actually had some tits to wrap up. It was quite funny seeing Cheryl covering up boobs she didn't even have.'

Cheryl soon began to issue demands.

'I don't need to be protected,' she said. 'I don't need to be in here with these faggots and kiddy fiddlers. I am a darling. No one wants to hurt me.'

The authorities agreed.

'She was a weird one,' the former officer said. 'Everyone seemed to like her and she had never been threatened. She proved to be someone who could hold her own, and honestly, she was that bloody ugly that no man was ever going to rape her.'

So Cheryl was moved.

'She ended up becoming quite popular,' the officer said. 'The guys really liked her. She would sew for them, she would clean their cells, and she became a mother figure for them.'

And she met Wayne, a heterosexual man who was serving life.

'Towards the end of her sentence she fell in love with an inmate called Wayne,' the former officer continued. 'He was a nice sort of bloke. He was really polite and a good style of man. And he wasn't gay, or at least that's what he said. He had a wife and kids outside and had never been in a homosexual relationship. So, yeah . . . I really don't know why he was attracted to her.'

Wayne was lonely. *And arse is arse, right?*

'I guess he needed a companion,' the former officer said. 'And I think she catered for a lot of his needs. She became quite a mother figure for a lot of men. She did a lot of things for him, and I guess he found it convenient.'

Cheryl and Wayne later announced themselves married. There was no certificate, of course, but they were husband and wife to anyone who asked.

'They were like an old couple,' the former officer said. 'They had a sensible relationship. It was really a normal relationship, considering it was in prison between a man and a man. They shared a cell together, and she took pride in doing all the chores, making the bed, cleaning and making cups of tea.'

The duo even became the first recipients of a double bed.

'They lived in the MSPC [Metropolitan Special Purpose Centre] at Long Bay,' the former officer continued. 'They had a two-out cell, and for some reason they had a double bed approved. I don't know *how* it got approved because only single beds are allowed in prison. But, regardless, they had one all the same. It wasn't a double bed as such, more a futon, so someone obviously pulled a shifty to get it to them.'

You would think both guards and prisoners would take offence to the so-called married couple living in the MSPC. If not for the fact that they were homosexual, geez . . . they had a double bed!

'It was funny because no one really blinked an eye at it or took issue with it,' the former officer said. 'Everyone knew they were a couple, and they didn't cause any trouble or bother anyone. It wasn't in anyone's face and they kept the sexual side private. It was never really a lovey-dovey type relationship. And everyone seemed to like Cheryl. He was the mother they never had.'

Wayne not only liked Cheryl, he loved her. Even after contracting HIV from his transsexual sweetheart, he took her back when she returned to Long Bay.

'It ended up killing him,' the former officer said. 'He died of AIDS while in custody.'

Cheryl suffered a similar fate.

'She died of a prescription drug overdose after she was transferred to Junee jail. The rumour is that they put all her medication in a bag when she was moved from Long Bay, and it ended up going into her cell. Anyway, she took it all at once and killed herself.'

8

WHAT THEY BECOME

Victoria Schembri

Our 'Model Inmate' survived four years in a maximum-security prison with some of Australia's most infamous female criminals. You've heard many of her stories. From meeting Katherine Knight to watching on as a woman had drugs ripped from her vagina as she slept, Schembri has seen it all.

Schembri agreed to reflect on her time in prison, to reveal what the experience did to her. To speak about the person she is now, and all the nightmares and scars. And also to reveal how the horror helped make her stronger.

These are Victoria's own words.

As the verdict was handed down, my innocence meant nothing.

I was now a convicted criminal for a crime I didn't commit.

My faith in the justice system had been torn apart. There was no justice. As I rocked there in the holding cells beneath Downing Centre at Surry Hills, my life flashed before my eyes. My daughters' faces, my son's face, just kept spinning as the tears that streamed down my face blurred my ability to see, let alone think straight. How was I, a mother, ever going to survive in a cell, surrounded by murderers, rapists, drug dealers, fraudsters and violent criminals?

I thought the nightmare would never end.

But I survived. I survived four years of horror and hardship. And it was courage and kindness that got me through. My heart told me not to waver and to stick to my morals and keep my integrity. I decided to stay true to and stick to my morals, even if it meant being bashed. Oh, and let me tell you, it happened. I was bashed – and more than once.

I remember thinking I would never make friends in jail or fit in. My knowledge of jail was that it was full of criminals. I was judgmental. I thought all of the women in jail were going to be scum. But I was so wrong. I would say about five per cent of people in jail are totally innocent of the crimes they have been convicted of. Many are there purely because their spouse was unable to be brought to justice. Some had no choice but to be behind these walls because the truth would see them dead.

I found myself drawn to these women, wanting to learn their stories, to share my story, and to prove that no matter what happened in life there was nothing in this world, not even a criminal conviction, that would define me. I wanted to show these women that they could judge me for not doing drugs, gambling or drinking alcohol, and even by how I looked – but I would not judge them.

Funny how that seems, right?

I was too pretty, and I was told that by the time I left these walls I was leaving with a scar on my pretty little face. Every day was lived in fear, and even more so when one of the girls told everyone who my ex-husband was. The world is so small; you never know who you will come across and where.

I stuck to myself, and more often than not found myself gravitating to the older ladies, the 'grandmas' and 'senior' women, like one of Australia's most notorious killers, Katherine Knight. Imagine meeting Katherine Knight for the first time. She looked at me and asked, 'Do you know who I am?' I had no idea who she was, but it didn't matter. I was here and I just wanted to get to the next day. I said no. After hearing her tell me who she was, I remember thinking how I wished I'd had it in me to do the same thing to my ex-husband, and I giggled out loud.

I made a friend with a woman who is portrayed by all the media as a cold-hearted, vicious woman. Grandma, as she was known, was kind but firm. She taught me how to play cards, and even how to crotchet. Yes, that's right, this woman who will never leave the walls of Silverwater Jail until the day she dies was humble and sweet. Grandma also helped me when times were tough and stood up for me when I became a topic of jailhouse gossip.

I also met women like Amnah Hamze, a well-known criminal. She is best known for having an uncle, Bassam Hamzy, who was running his drug empire from behind the walls of Lithgow Jail. This girl had so many stories of the craziness that was her life in jail. I struggled believing much of it, but it was all true. I found that the less I cared about why or what these woman were here for, the more they gravitated or repelled from me.

There were women who talked about ripping off their companies for millions of dollars. Many of them were using stolen gold bullion to trade while in jail. I remember being so appalled. These women were so narcissistic that there was no remorse, and the schemes and conniving behaviour was so repulsive to me. I'd rather share my time with a drug mule.

Some days I thought I was going insane. And maybe I was. I also feared I would be killed. One thing that helped get me through was kindness. I realised there were things I could do for these women that would help them feel good. I had talents at my disposal that could help me stay safe and alive. I owned two hair and beauty salons before I was sent to jail. And I had skills I could use inside. I became an in-house beautician for many of Australia's worst criminals

It is amazing how by simply removing the safety bar from a razor I could create new hairstyles and give these women a sense of self and even an identity. I even helped them do the Avon orders to ensure they picked the right colour make-up or hair dyes to create the look they wanted. I used dinner platers to do their hair foils.

Each day would pass in a haze, and the only thing that kept me sane was writing in my journal, colouring in, studying and writing poems. As each day faded from one to the next, so too did fear, anxiety, happiness, sadness, self-loathing, depression, denial, grief, anger, disbelief – and too many more emotions to name on the roller-coaster that is life behind those walls.

There came a point where, after being bashed in medium security and transferred back to maximum for my own safety – because I refused to name the perpetrator – that I met a woman I refer to as my soul sister. This lady and I became the best of friends, and to this day we remain so.

In jail we exercised together, worked together, shared the story of our lives and families together, and we even shared a cell together. We read the Bible, prayed and went to church together. We loved to write poetry, do art and even gave pottery a go. When one was feeling down, the other was there to listen or cry, and even make the other laugh. I soon realised that just because I was locked up no one could take my happiness away from me but me.

And let me tell you about the food. Oh, it was shit. For all the TV shows that talk about fresh meals and *blah, blah, blah* that inmates get, *pfft!* We are treated like sub-humans. The food is inedible, and God forbid you have an allergy! The number of girls who had allergic reactions, even anaphylaxis, was a joke. It was more often than not that the safest choice was to go without food. My weight plummeted to 48kg at one point from lack of food.

Today I look back on those four years and it still feels like a nightmare. The difference is that the horror is over. But I still have nightmares.

I am thankful for my experience behind those walls. It made me stronger in spirit, and yet I am still a marshmallow of emotions. It made me more determined and even less judgmental, which is a word I would never have actually used to describe myself, considering I was pretty accepting in the first place. It showed me just how naive I was to the reality of the real world I had never encountered before, and most of all it taught me that the humility I held onto from my days in the limelight was a virtue that I would hold close to this very day.

I learned to appreciate the leaves in the tree blowing in the wind and the birds singing – even the sound of traffic in the distance was music to my ears. The ability to appreciate the simplest of things was magnified like a telescopic lens. I realised just how lucky I was. I actually learned what it was to have nothing!

My new partner, John, showed me unconditional love by staying by my side for the whole four years. He also kept my children well. He could have walked away – we had only been together for 18 months – but he didn't, and we found true love.

Today I am a women's empowerment speaker, and a sexual health educator with a team of over 60 women.

I raise money for cancer each year and help women realise that loving yourself is more important than loving society's version of what magazines say you should be happy looking like. I've used my experience to help women.

My life has been a roller-coaster of unfortunate events, but thanks to each and every person I have met, this mother – and now grandmother – will always sparkle a little brighter.

Read on for an extract from
Australia's Toughest Prisons: Inmates

MAKING A MURDERER
Minda and Kariong

Uzzles

Flick. Nothing. *Flick.* Nothing. *Flick* . . . Finally the flint sparked the butane, sending the flame into the unfurled aluminum foil.

'Nah, not yet,' said the kid holding both the lighter and the sandwich wrapper he'd rescued from the bin. 'Wait. I'll tell ya when.'

The other kid – the one with the sipping straw stuck to his lip – pulled back. 'Yeah, sweet,' he said, nodding.

The flame turned the foil black, and the brown blob sitting on top began to bubble.

'Now,' said the cook. 'Rip in.'

Sitting on the concrete, a toilet the only thing between him and his newest mate, he leant in and sucked, aiming the end of the straw above the bubbling blob. He heaved into the smoke and inhaled with all his might.

'Hold it,' said the cook. 'Hold it in for as long as you can.'

So he did. Not daring to exhale until his face was red-raw from the strain.

Pffffft.

Smoke spewed into the air as his lungs contracted explosively.

He waited.

Nothing.

'This ain't doing shit,' he coughed.

And then it came. The hit. The oblivion.

He smiled, not knowing he would soon be an addict . . . *A druggie at the age of 13.*

This is the shocking story of how a juvenile detention centre turned a child into a killer. How bashings, brawls and the ever-present badness of a house of horrors made a murderer.

And it all began with a spot of heroin, smuggled into the Minda Juvenile Justice Centre in south-west Sydney by a 16-year-old.

'I had a mate from school, and he was in there the same time as me,' said Dave Hooker, now 38, who bravely went on the record to tell his sad, sickening and soon-to-turn sinister story. 'He came up to me one day and asked me if I wanted some "uzzles". I didn't even know what the fuck it was. That was what they called H [heroin] in there. No idea why, but that's what they called it. I don't know how he got it, but he had it and I was up for anything.'

Hooker, a 13-year-old car thief and Minda's newest resident, nodded and said, 'Sure, why not?' Amid the monsters, most aged 18, more men than boys, sucking back on heroin was better than sitting alone and thinking about *when* – not *if* – he would be bashed for his shoes.

'He told me to meet him down by the toilets, so I did,' Hooker continued. 'He put the shit on the foil and gave me a straw and said, "Here you go." He sparked it up for me and I had a toke. I had a smoke afterwards while he was having a go. We went back and forth until it was all gone.'

The fear of being bashed, raped or just bloody bored was sucked from Hooker's body by the burning brown. Numb, the teenager walked out into the yard. He felt nothing . . . well, until he felt sick.

'I walked out into the yard and started spewing,' Hooker continued. 'I had been feeling smashed, awesome. There was nothing in my head. And then I started chucking all over the concrete. Blokes were looking at me like I was on fire or something. I was like, *What the fuck is this? What did I do that for?* I felt terrible.'

But there is no prize for guessing where this story goes. Like all soon-to-be addicts, he forgot about the chunks that had flown from his mouth and splattered onto the concrete floor, about the horrible headaches and the shakes he suffered throughout the night.

He went back for more, of course.

'I was around H all the time after that,' Hooker said. 'I would take it whenever it was around.'

So how does a 13-year-old get his hands on the world's most addictive, destructive drug while in a state-run juvenile centre? A place where he had been sent to 'learn his lesson', to reform and rehabilitate?

'It was easy to get in,' Hooker said. 'My mate was an Asian, and it was the other older Asian blokes who were giving it to him. I ended up meeting those older boys too, and they started giving it to me. I did it whenever I could get it. Sometimes it would be once a week. Sometimes it would be once every second day. It just depended how much was around and whose turn it was to get some.'

The infamous Sydney Vietnamese street gang called '5T', or the T's for short, were supplying heroin to the juvenile offenders, according to the kid who would become a teenage junkie.

5T was a murderous outfit that imported heroin from South-East Asia and flooded Sydney with the drug during the 1990s from their Cabramatta base.

'The T's were coming in and giving it to their younger brothers,' Hooker continued. 'The older boys would come in to visit and give it to them. It started becoming more regular from the time I got there, and eventually it was coming in every week.'

5T, cashed up from their roaring drug trade, handed the H over to their family members for free. They didn't know or care whether or not their brothers were taking the drug themselves or using it as currency.

'I never had to pay for it,' Hooker said. 'Not during my stint in Minda, anyway. I probably would have never become an addict if I wasn't getting it for nothing, because I *had* nothing. But in that place, at that time, we were all mates and we shared what we had. They were getting plenty, so they were happy to pass it around. It went that way until I got out.'

But this is where the story takes a darker turn – in Minda, with a 13-year-old sucking heroin through a straw next to a 'shitta', one night after being thrown in a cold, lonely cell, with nothing but a bed, a pillow and a blanket.

Huaraches

Hooker's highway to heroin had begun on a truck.

'Nice shoes, bro,' the Aboriginal boy, aged about 16, said. 'Nikes, hey? Yep, they'll be fuckin' mine by the end of the day.'

Hooker looked past the chains that connected the constricting cuffs and down to his Nike Huaraches planted on the bus floor.

He had bought 'the latest and greatest' in footwear not long before he stole a car and led police on a high-speed chase from Bankstown to Penrith. He'd used the money he'd stolen in an armed robbery to buy the $250 kicks.

'Yeah, we'll see about that,' Hooker replied.

The older kid, flanked by a posse of big boys who appeared to be his mates, smiled.

'Yep,' he fired. 'We sure will.'

Trying to be all tough and terrifying, Hooker stared at the mob as the truck rattled its way to Lidcombe – home of the Minda Juvenile Justice Centre.

'Obviously I was scared,' he recalled. 'You have that fear in ya – especially being just 13 – but I knew I couldn't be weak. I'd heard shit like this went on, and I was expecting it.

'I had already been printed and strip searched at the police station. I guess that's when you start getting a bit nervous. I was then transferred into a prison truck, and that is pretty shit. Once you get in the truck you're cuffed up and can't see shit. That was pretty bad.'

Then came the threat.

'There were a few Aboriginals on the truck, and I just thought, *Oh fuck*. You always hear about the Abos and how bad they are in jail. They want your shoes and all that sort of shit. They are pretty well known for sticking together in numbers and for cracking people.

'I thought, *Here we go. I'm about to have my first fight.* I had the latest Huaraches on at the time and thought, *No way are they getting these.*

And, yep . . . they tried it on.

The taunts and threats went back and forth until the bus stopped at Minda – the 'junior jail' that has housed the worst juvenile offenders in New South Wales since 1966. No doubt some of them were now buried in nearby Rookwood Cemetery – the famous graveyard a frightfully fitting neighbor for this living hell.

'When I got out of the truck, they handcuffed me to one of the Abos who wanted my shoes,' Hooker said. 'They split us into groups of two so they could do the searches, and that's when you start to feel really vulnerable.'

Hooker wasn't just worried about copping a hiding from

the older, stronger kid linked to him by the cold chain. No . . . He was even more terrified of the guards and their *plastic latex gloves.*

'Get 'em off,' the officer said. 'Everything. Take every item of clothing off right now, including your socks and shoes.'

Not so bad, Hooker initially thought. *Same as the cop shop.*

'But then he screamed at me to bend over,' Hooker said, recalling the horrifying experience. 'And he went right on with it, looking in my arse, grabbing at my balls. It was fucking terrible, only being a kid. And I don't think they were just searching us for gear . . . I think it was a bit of a scare tactic as well.'

And it worked.

'I remember walking into the main jail after being searched, and everything just became narrow,' he said. 'It was like I had tunnel vision. I kept my eyes down and looked at nothing. And I said nothing until they screamed my name. That was a reality check too, because no one called me by my name. I hadn't heard my own name for a while, because on the streets I had my street name. A nickname.'

The reception guard fired off a full magazine lode of questions: *What's your date of birth? Do you have any gang affiliations? Do you have any tattoos? Are any of your co-offenders incarcerated here? Do you have any enemies that might be here?*

'I remember looking into a wing while he was asking me shit,' Hooker continued.

'And I could see all these perspex windows. Behind them I could see all these blokes. They were yelling out, screaming and banging on the glass.'

Yep. Now he was scared. Shitting bricks.

'The boys in there were aged anywhere from ten to 18,' Hooker said. 'But when I walked in, all the guys I'd first seen were 17, so to me they were men. I was still a little kid and they were all developed and quite big. I remember looking at the Islander boys – they were just fucking huge. I started worrying then. I was sure I was going to have to fight them.'

A guard screamed his name: 'David Hooker!' The name he hadn't heard since the day he'd quit school. *Primary school.*

'He handed me a pile of clothes,' Hooker said. 'They were all black. Others guys had been given other colours, and I wondered what it was all about. It was a colour code. Whatever colour they gave you determined where you went. Black meant I was going to a wing called Kendall.'

The rest of the new inmates were given different colours and sent off to four other wings: McKellar, Transit, Talbot or Lawson.

'Hookzy!' a boy screamed as he entered the wing. 'What the fuck are you doing here?'

The familiar face forced out the fear.

'I was relieved straightaway because all these blokes I grew up with on the street were there,' Hooker said. 'I can't remember how many, but there were a few, and right then and there I knew I'd be sweet. They were older than me, and tough too. You have all your little groups and gangs in Minda. And when I got put in, most of the blokes were from Bankstown, which is where I'm from. It was the closest jail to Bankstown, so that's where all the boys from round there went.'

Maybe this won't be so bad? Hooker thought. *Maybe I won't be killed after all?*

'The boys pulled me aside and told me it was still a fucking madhouse,' Hooker said. 'They told me you get fucked up big-time if you didn't follow the rules.'

Then they gave him the prison code – the unwritten laws that might just save his life. *Or end it . . .*

'They told me what not to do and what I should be doing,' Hooker said. 'First up, they told me everything in jail was political. They said there are the blacks, there are the whites, there are the Asians, there are the Islanders, and there are the Lebos.

'They also told me some of the guys were linked to some pretty big street gangs, like 5T and all that kind of shit.'

Hooker stood with his mates and they looked around the wing. One pointed. 'See him?'

Hookz nodded.

'Don't fuck with him. And see that bloke?'

Hookz nodded again.

'5T.'

'They told me who the big people were and who I shouldn't take on,' Hooker recalled of the briefing. 'They also told me not to give anyone up, and I was just like, *Shit, I know that. That's a street rule.* The rest of it was pretty simple. They basically said stick with us and you'll be sweet. They said keep to yourself when you aren't with us, and don't fuck with anyone we've pointed out. And if anything goes wrong, we'll sort it out. Shit like that.

'I didn't think anything of it back then – it all seemed like a bit of fun – but looking back now it was pretty hectic. We were just kids, but we were already into prison codes. Blood in, blood out – you know?'

But for now he didn't care. All that mattered was that he had his boys, had his Huaraches. Everything would be sweet.

Or so he thought . . .

Bashed, Broken and a Bum Full of Tobacco

'Where the fuck is it, *Hooker*?' yelled the guard, spit spraying as he screamed at the kid.

He had unlocked the heavy metal door and launched into the cell – a 4 metre by 3 metre concrete room.

'Where is what?' Hooker replied as he sprang to attention. 'I ain't got shit, sir.'

The guard looked around. It was difficult to hide anything in a place like this. Scarily similar to any cell in an adult jail, light came in through a small barred window covered in perspex peppered with breeze holes. The door was solid steel with an 'observation window' cut into the middle.

The fresh inmate only had a bed, a toilet and a small shelf to keep his belongings . . . but it was bare. The only thing Hooker owned in Minda was now between his arse cheeks . . .

'Someone had slid me a ciggie under the door,' Hooker recalled. 'We used to tie shit to cotton and push it across the floor and under the door with a stick or something. On this occasion the officer actually saw it being dragged across the floor. He came in to have a go at me and I told him I didn't have shit. I told him to prove it, but he couldn't find it because I had it in my arse cheeks. In my "safe" . . . *ha*. That's what we called it.'

'Bullshit,' the guard had said. 'I saw you pull something under the door.'

Hooker shook his head, a giant smirk plastered on his face. Soon the officer had a companion. Another burly beast barged into the room and stood just in front of the open door.

'Bend over, you little shit,' said the accuser. 'Drop your dacks, cunt, and spread your cheeks.'

Oh no.

'Fuck off, you faggot,' Hooker said defiantly. He pointed at the officer guarding the door. 'Go look in your mate's arse if that's your thing.'

Whoosh!

The guard grabbed the boy – all 45kg of him – and threw him across the room.

Bang!

Hooker's tiny frame slammed into the wall, all brick and concrete render.

The guard who'd tossed him rushed forward, as did the other loitering guard.

They both grabbed the kid before hoisting him, with only the slightest effort, two feet into the air. And then they shook him – *up, down, left, right*. Hookzy was a ragdoll whose stitches stretched as he was swung, slapped and eventually dropped on his head.

'They came over and threw me around,' Hooker said. 'They were trying to make [the tobacco] drop, but I was clenching my arse for the life of me to keep it in there.'

His pants had been ripped off. He was all arse, balls and swinging cock. They shook harder.

Whack!

'I cracked one of them in the mouth,' Hooker continued. 'I wasn't about to take that shit. I didn't really care about being caught with the gear, but to be hurled around in the nude by two faggots was just humiliating.'

The officer reeled, surprised by the force of the blow.

Can a 13-year-old really hit that hard?

He didn't stop to consider his question before returning payment – with interest, of course.

'He didn't like it when I hit him,' Hooker said. 'He was a big unit, probably about 110kg. And he flogged the shit out of me.'

Umphhh! Umphhh!

It started with two body blows, but Hooker was punched in the face after he hit the officer again.

'Once I started throwing, the other bloke came in too. They gave me a hiding, smashing my face in before putting me in a headlock, trying to choke me out.'

And boy, did it hurt.

'I was a mess. I was sent to the hospital with "self-inflicted injuries". *Ha!* I had bruises everywhere – my arms, legs, even footprints on the side of my ribs. You could see the shoe marks from where they had stomped me with their boots. My whole neck was bruised from the strangling they gave me.'

His face, too, was swollen and covered in blood.

What did the nurse do, aside from treat his wounds? *Nothing.*

'I couldn't say anything,' Hooker recalled of the incident. 'I just had to cop it. I couldn't dob, and no one who worked there put the screws in.'

The only thing Hooker could do was issue a threat of his own. As the instigating officer dragged him from the floor, the belted, bruised and busted kid made a bold threat. A brave promise considering he could have been flogged – there and then – again.

'I told him I was going to upend him the next time he opened the door. I told him he wouldn't see it coming.'

The officer laughed . . .

Sadly, at Minda (and, to be fair, other juvenile detention institutions around Australia) bashings were common. Another former 'juvie' confirmed the brutality of the junior jails.

'The guards would come in and give you a flogging,' said the reformed 42-year-old, who asked not to be named. 'Some of them would just throw you around . . . or that's how it would start, anyway. It would be verbal at first. They would say, "Shut the fuck up or we'll come in and smash you."

'And us, being the rowdy little fuckers we were, would say, "Yeah, come in. Bring it on." They would then open up the door. Four of them would come in. Two would give you the hiding, one would be at the door, and one would be in the corridor. The guy in the hall would just be shutting everyone else up, and the one at the door would stop anyone else from getting in.

'They'd throw you around and it would just egg us on. We would start throwing punches and they would throw them back.'

He recalled one particular bashing he'd received in Minda.

His crime? *Talking.*

'They said they were going to give me a hiding one day because I was talking too much. I told them to fuck off – I would talk whenever I wanted.'

He got belted, *of course.*

As for Hooker and his brave threat? The 13-year-old and his promise to 'upend' the guard who'd left him black and blue but failed to find the tobacco stuffed in his arse?

'He eventually came back to my cell,' Hooker said. 'And, yep . . . I got him.'

His revenge did not come swiftly, but it did come – with a thunderous crack to the face.

'I waited a while so I could build up a few points for good behaviour,' Hooker continued. 'When you had enough points they gave you things, like books and maybe a TV. I ended up with a radio. It had three of those big D batteries in it. So I put them in a sock.'

He waited, waited and waited some more. Eventually Mr 'Drop-Your-Dacks-Cunt' entered his cell. And he copped a half-kilo cannonball to the face.

'He came through the door and I swung it at him. I think I broke his jaw.'

About the Author

James Phelps is an award-winning senior reporter for the *Daily* and *Sunday Telegraph* in Sydney. He began as an overnight police rounds reporter before moving into sport, where he became one of Australia's best news-breaking rugby league reporters.

James became News Australia's Chief National Motorsports writer and travelled the world chasing F1 stories, as well as becoming Australia's No. 1 V8 Supercar reporter. James is also a senior feature writer for the *Sunday Telegraph*.

Following the bestselling *Dick Johnson: The Autobiography of a True-Blue Aussie Sporting Legend*, James returned to his roots to delve into the criminal underworld with *Australia's Hardest Prison: Inside the Walls of Long Bay Jail*; *Australia's Most Murderous Prison: Behind the Walls of Goulburn Jail* and *Australia's Toughest Prisons: Inmates*. James is a twice V8 Supercar media award-winner and a former News Awards 'Young Journalist of the Year' and 'Sport Reporter of the Year', as well as a Kennedy Awards finalist for 'Sports Reporter of the Year'.